Business And Consumer Financial Answers

Business Financing Commence 1.1

Martex E-Technology LLC

iUniverse, Inc.
New York Lincoln Shanghai

Business And Consumer Financial Answers
Business Financing Commence 1.1

iUniverse books may be ordered through booksellers or by contacting:

iUniverse
2021 Pine Lake Road, Suite 100
Lincoln, NE 68512
www.iuniverse.com
1-800-Authors (1-800-288-4677)

ISBN-13: 978-0-595-38940-7 (pbk)
ISBN-13: 978-0-595-83324-5 (ebk)
ISBN-10: 0-595-38940-6 (pbk)
ISBN-10: 0-595-83324-1 (ebk)

Printed in the United States of America

Contents

EXECUTIVE SUMMARY

Business versality from desk and market research carried out by various commercial businesses is a potential improvement segment of the economy market.

The professional, who want to explore new business acumen to acquire and administer material and information resources in a manner which instills public trust and accomplishes the set task giving by the organization is not having their needs properly meet.

These adventurous professionals find it difficult to get good reliable and creatively products and services.

Martex E-Technology LLC timely and effective strategic evaluation believes that by concentrating on one market segment, and geographic destinations, the significant superior result driven analysis and tools capability will meet their desired requirements.

Write Action Plan Notes

EMPLOYEE RESOURCE

The detail expectations of employees and answers of their questions of the company.

The consistency of an employee mission communicates indispensable company policies and practices.

Building blocks of employee resource policies conveys a broader sense of the company's mission.

Write Action Plan Notes

BUSINESS FINANCING

We have selected a relatively extensive achievement for the start-up, expanding and leasing companies in connections to short-term and long-term financing.

Set specific, measurable standards for the results you require are mentioned in details in the business financing commence 1.1, pages 1 and all to follow.

The business operations organization is detailed with specific processes set to meet your interim and deadlines capital finance.

Write Action Plan Notes

START-UP CAPITAL

LOAN GURANTEES

The SBA provides capital to small business in terms of guaranteed major percentage (%) of the loans to small business

SBA's 7(a) General Business Loan Guarantee

The 7(a) program enables guaranteed loans to small business disadvantaged in capital.

The program runs through private sector lenders with an SBA guarantee.

SBA MICROLOANS

SBA provides access to credit up to $35,000 at favorable terms and conditions through accepted nonprofit community based lenders (intermediaries).

The average loan size is about $10,500.

SBA CERTIFIED DEVELOPMENT COMPANY (504) LOAN PROGRAM

Nationwide, SBA provides growing businesses with long term, fixed rate financing for major fixed assets, such as land and buildings.

There are about 270 CDCs nationwide.

SBA EXPRESSLOANS

A new tool that makes it faster and easier for lenders to provide small loans of $150,000 or less, with approvals in less than 36 hours and less government paperwork.

Lenders are not required to take collateral for loans up to $25,000. Lenders may use their existing collateral policy for loans over $25,000 up to $150,000.

Write Action Plan Notes

SBA's LOWDOC LOAN

The new LowDoc is streamlined for success, quicker SBA turnaround, and easier. It's a one-page application. If you need up to $150,000 in credit with an 85% guarantee, this is the right tool.

SBA REVOLVING WORKING CAPITAL LINES

Working capital loans to help small businesses meet their short-term revolving working capital needs.

Under this tool, the available programs available are as follows:

- **Export Working Capital (EWCP):**

Designed to provide short-term working capital to exporters.

SBA guarantees EWCP loan requests of $1,111,111 or less while loan requests over $1,111,111 may be processed through the Export-Import Bank. When an EWCP loan is combined with an international trade loan, the SBA's exposure can go up to $1.25 million.

The proceeds of an EWCP loan must be used to finance the working capital needs associated with a single or multiple transactions of the exporter.

The SBIC division of the SBA provides start-up capital to companies completing product development and initial marketing. Companies may be in the process of organizing or they may be in business for a year or less, but have not sold their product commercially. Usually such firms will have made market studies, assembled key management, developed a business plan and are ready to do business.

Write Action Plan Notes

SBA PLP and CLP Lenders by State

Alabama

CIT Small Business Lending Corp.

PNB 117731 Montgomery Hwy.
Birmingham, AL 35216
Contact: Michael Vance, Regional Account Manager
Tel: 205-824-2810
Fax: 205-824-2811

Compass Bank

P. O. Box 10566
Birmingham, AL 35296
Contact: John Bates, Vice President
Tel: 205-297-3346
Fax: 205-297-7672

G.E. Capital Small Business Finance Corp.

2090 Columbiana Road Suite 200
Birmingham, AL 35216
Contact: Elise Dubas, Executive Vice President
Tel: 205-443-0377
Fax: 205-443-0303

SouthTrust Bank of Alabama, N.A.

360 Interstate Pkwy. N Suite 500

Atlanta, GA 30339
Contact: Juan Lago, Group Vice President
Fax: 770-678-3770
Fax: 770-678-3779

Wachovia SBA Lending, Inc.

d/b/a Wachovia Small Business Capital
1 Perimeter Park South Suite 100 North
Birmingham, AL 35243
Contact: Sam A. Renta, Jr., Business Development Officer
Tel: 205-982-7900
Fax: 205-982-7904

Alaska

First National Bank of Alaska

Key Bank of Alaska

Northrim Bank

Wells Fargo

Denali State Bank

First Bank

Business Lenders, LLC

Business Loan Center, Inc.

Write Action Plan Notes

CIT Small Business Lending Corporation

Arizona

Alliance Bank of Arizona

7373 North Scottsdale Road, Suite A-195
Scottsdale, Arizona 85253
Tel: 480-998-6500

Arizona Business Bank

2700 North Central Ave., #210
Phoenix, Arizona 85004
Tel: 602-240-2704

Bank of America

201 East Washington St.
Phoenix, Arizona 85004
Tel: 480-827-6582

Bank One Arizona

1515 West 14th St., Bldg. C
Tempe, Arizona 85281
Tel: 888-536-3722

Bank of the Southwest

7910 South Kyrene Road #108
Tempe, Arizona 85284
Tel: 480-346-4621

Bank of the West

1702 East Highland Ave.#318
Phoenix, Arizona 85016
Tel: 602-235-9400

Borrego Springs Bank, N.A.

P.O. Box 10123
Glendale, Arizona 85318
Tel: 602-291-1440

Borrego Springs Bank, N.A.

5055 East Broadway, C-214
Tucson, Arizona 85711
Tel: 520-745-5131

Arkansas

Amresco Independence Funding, Inc

Tel: 214-953-8400

Arkansas Capital Group

Tel: 800-216-7237

Bank of America

All Locations

Bank of the West

Tel: 530-582-3803

Write Action Plan Notes

Bank United

Tel: 713-543-7063

Business Loan Center, Inc

Tel: 800-690-9089

Cit Small Business Lending Corp

Tel: 973-355-7524

Commercial Capital Corporation

Tel: 212-719-0002

Compass Bank

Tel: 972-735-3577

Elk Horn Bank And Trust

Tel: 870-246-5811

First Union Small Business Capital

Tel: 800-722-3066

First Western Sblc, Inc

Tel: 972-349-3209

G E Capital Small Business Fin. Corp

Tel: 901-762-4324

Heller First Capital Corp

Tel: 800-347-6430

Regions Bank

All Locations

Zions National Bank

Tel: 801-887-4277

Arkansas National Bank

706 S. Walton Blvd.
P. O. Box 699
Bentonville, AR 72712
Tel: 501-271-280

City National Bank

1222 Rogers Avenue
P. O. Box 47
Fort Smith, AR 72901
Tel: 501-785-2811

California

Bank of Alameda

2130 Otis
Alameda, CA 94501
Tel: 510-769-9338

Bank of America CDB

c/o 1456, 300 S Harbor Blvd.
Anaheim, CA 92805
Tel: 800-263-2055

Write Action Plan Notes

GE Capital Small Business Finance Corp.

2400 E Katella Ave., Ste. #800
Anaheim, CA 92806
Tel: 714-456-9400

Arcata Economic Development Corporation

100 Ericson Court, Suite 100

Arcata, CA 95521

Tel: 707-822-4616

International Bank of California

17100 Pioneer Blvd
Artesia, CA 90701
Tel: 562-860-8118
Fax: 562-467-0250

Auburn National Bank

412 Auburn Folsom Road
Auburn, CA 95603
Tel: 530-887-8182

San Joaquin Bank

4600 California Ave.
Bakersfield, CA 93389
Tel: 661-281-0325
Fax: 661-281-0333

Bank of America

Community Development Bank
Tel: 800-263-2055
http://www.bankofamerica.com

U.S. Bank

Tel: 800-698-8980

Imperial Bank

Tel: 916-443-3293

California Federal

Tel: 707-578-7630

Money Store Investment Corp.

Tel: 800-722-3066
http://www.themoneystore.com

Bank of Walnut Creek

Tel: 925-932-5353
http://www.bowc.com

District of Columbia

AMRESCO Independence Funding, Inc.

Mr. Charles P. Bell
President
Tel: 214-953-8908
Fax: 214-758-5260

Adams National Bank, The

Ms. Kathryn Speakman
Vice President
Tel: 202-466-4090
Fax: 202-835-3871

Write Action Plan Notes

Allfirst Bank

Mr. Calvin L. Garlic
Senior Vice President
Tel: 410-244-4007
Fax: 410-244-4070

Bank of America, National
Association

Mr. Russell G. Sardina
Senior Vice President
Tel: 916-861-6729
Fax: 916-861-6779

Branch Banking and Trust
Company

Mr. David Mann
Vice President
Tel: 336-733-3441
Fax: 336-733-3419

Business Lenders LLC

Mr. Penn J. Ritter
President & CEO
Tel: 860-244-9202
Fax: 860-527-0884

Business Loan Center, Inc.

Mr. Deryl Schuster
President Mid America Div
Tel: 800-722-5626
Fax: 316-263-4391

CIT Small Business Lending
Corporation

Mr. Chris Lehnes
VP-Business Development
Tel: 973-422-6004
Fax: 973-422-6130

California Center Bank

Mr. K. Jason Kim
Vice President & Manager
Tel: 213-637-9622
Fax: 213-427-6080

Citibank, Federal Savings
Bank

Mr. Samuel D. Kaplan
Senior Credit Officer
Tel: 636-256-5925
Fax: 636-256-5549

Georgia

Athens First Bank & Trust

c/o Synovus SBA Lending
4159 Mill Street
P.O. Box 2039
Covington, GA 30014
Contact: Kim Hartbarger
Tel: 770-385-3411
Fax: 678-625-1799
Email:
kimhartbarger@sti.synovus.com

Atlantic States Bank

2140 Satellite Boulevard
Duluth, GA 30097
Contact: Dana Little

Write Action Plan Notes

Tel: 678-473-7632
Fax: 678-473-9919

Bank of America

3350 Riverwood Pkwy, 11th Floor
Atlanta, GA 30339
Contact: Vicki Molinari
Tel: 770-850-5547
Fax: 770-850-5543

Bank of North Georgia

c/o Synovus SBA Lending
4159 Mill Street
P.O. Box 2039
Covington, GA 30014
Tel: 770-385-3411
Fax: 678-625-1799
email:
kimhartbarger@sti.synovus.com

Branch Banking & Trust Company

5901-C Peachtree-Dunwoody RD
Suite 420
Atlanta, GA 30328
Contact: Vincent Dailey
Tel: 770-522-0582
Fax: 770-551-8781

Business Development

Corporation of Georgia, Inc,
1450 S. Johnson Ferry Road

Atlanta, GA 30319
Contact: Tom Dorman
Tel: 404-475-6011
Fax: 404-475-6013

Business Loan Express

3675 Cloudland Drive, NW
Atlanta, GA 30327
Contact: Rebecca Grant
Tel: 404-995-7025
Fax: 404-816-2010

Hawaii

Bank of Hawaii

P.O. Box 2900
Honolulu, HI 96846
Tel: 808-537-8568

Central Pacific Bank

P.O. Box 3590
Honolulu, HI 96811
Tel: 808-544-0605

City Bank

P.O. Box 3709
Honolulu, HI 96811
Tel: 808-535-2460

First Hawaiian Bank

P.O. Box 3200
Honolulu, HI 96847

Write Action Plan Notes

Hawaii National Bank

P. O. Box 3740

Honolulu, HI 96812

Tel: 808-528-7823

Business Loan Center, Inc.

121 West Dewey Street, Suite 210
Wichita, Kansas 67202
Tel: 316-263-3232

Idaho

Bank of America

421 N. Cole Road
Boise, Idaho 83704

Bank of Commerce

1455 Northgate Mile
P. O. Box 1887
Idaho Falls, Idaho 83401

Bank of the West

9140 W. Emerald
Boise, Idaho 83704

Citizens Community Bank

280 South Arthur
P. O. Box 1689
Pocatello, Idaho 83204

Illinois

Great Lakes Bank

11346 S. Cicero
Alsip, IL 60808
Contact: Gary Wesner
Tel: 708-283-7266
Fax: 708-388-1990

Old Second National Bank of Aurora)

37 S. River Street
Aurora, IL 60507
Contact: John Medernach
Tel: 630-906-5482
Fax: 630-892-2412

Union Planters

7650 Magna Drive
Belleville, IL 62223
Contact: Ed Broderhausen
Tel: 800-444-7041
Fax: 618-239-4887

Greater Chicago Bank

219 S. Mannheim Road
Bellwood, IL 60104
Contact: George Anderson, Senior Vice President
Tel: 708-547-3671
Fax: 708-547-4069

Robert J. Foy, President

Tel: 773-465-7555
Fax: 773-465-4598

Write Action Plan Notes

Old National Bank

509 S. University
Carbondale, IL 62901
Greg Ingram, Vice President
Tel: 618-457-3381
Fax: 618-529-7574

Bank Illinois

100 W. University
Champaign, IL 61824
Contact: Wes Curtis, Senior
Vice President
Tel: 217-351-2759
Fax: 217-351-2771

Bank of Charleston (CLP)

621 Lincoln Avenue
Charleston, IL 61920
Contact: Don Mapes, Vice
President
Tel: 217-348-8131
Fax: 217-348-8210

Indiana

Wells Fargo Bank

Indianapolis Office
10401 N Meridian Street,
46290
Tel: 317-581-6218

Allied Capital SBLC
Corporation

8888 Keystone Crossing,
Suite 1300, 46240
Tel: 317-581-8568

Unizan Bank, N.A.,

8425 Woodfield Crossing
Blvd., Suite 100, 46240
Tel: 317-469-7575

Wachovia Small Business
Capital

3815 River Crossing
Parkway, Suite 100, 46240
Tel: 317-566-2140

National City Bank of
Indiana

One National City Center,
700E, 46255
Tel: 317-267-8887

Bank One, Indiana, N.A.,

111 Monument Circle, Suite
971, 46277
Tel: 317-321-3000

Iowa

Iowa Bank

300 N 2nd Street, 52031-1232
Tel: 563-872-5515

Write Action Plan Notes

U.S. Bank

201 Jefferson, 52601-1088
Tel: 319-752-2761

Wells Fargo Bank NA

302 Main Street, 50613
Tel: 319-273-8800

Farmers & Merchants Savings Bank

4020 First Ave. NE, 52402
Tel: 319-366-8681

Kansas

Farmers Bank & Trust, N.A.
1017 Harrison

Great Bend, KS 67530
Karesa Harrison, Vice President
Tel: 316-792-2411
Fax: 316-793-8526

INTRUST Bank, NA & branches
Box 1

Wichita, KS 67201
John J. Luerding, Executive Vice President
Tel: 316-383-1266
Fax: 316-383-1665

Emprise Bank, N.A.

Box 400
Hays, KS 67601
Randy Walker, Vice President
Tel: 785-625-6595
Fax: 785-625-9561

Tyco Capital Small Business Lending Corp.

12120 State Line Rd., Suite 157
Leawood, KS 66209
Paul Jokerst, Regional Accounts Manager
Tel: 816-941-2090
Fax: 816-941-0081

Transamerica Small Business Capital, Inc.

9393 W. 110th Street, Suite 534
Overland Park, KS 66210
Clark A. Churchill, Vice President
Tel: 913-451-6776
Fax: 913-451-6782

GE Capital Small Business Finance

818 E. Orme
Wichita, KS 67211
Brent Koehn
Tel: 316-303-3515
Cell: 316-706-0359

Write Action Plan Notes

Kentucky

PNC Bank Kentucky Inc

Citizens Plaza 5th Floor
Louisville KY 40296
Contact: Mr. Don Gossman
Tel: 502-581-2038

National City Bank

P O BOX 36000
Louisville KY 40233-6000
Contact: Mr. Alan Kissel
(LOUISVILLE & W. KY)
Tel: 502-581-6394
Contact: MR. David Simpson
(CENTRAL & E. KY)
Tel: 606-238-1027
Contact: Randy Goode
(Exporting Loan Officer)
Tel: 502-581-4086

Maine

First National Bank of Bar
Harbor

102 Main Street
Bar Harbor, ME 04609

Tel: 207-288-3341
Fax: 207-288-2451

Fleet Bank of ME

1 City Center
Portland, ME 04104

Tel: 207-874-5000
Fax: 207-874-5117

KeyBank National Association

179 John Roberts Road
So Portland, ME 04106
Tel: 207-842-1051
Fax: 207-842-1050

Kennebunk Savings Bank

104 Main Street
Kennebunk, ME 04043
Tel: 207-985-4903
Fax: 207-984-6034

Merrill Merchants Bank

201 Main Street
Bangor, ME 04402
Tel: 207-942-4800
Fax: 207-942-9255

Northeast Bank, F.S.B.

232 Center Street
Auburn, ME 04210
Tel: 207-777-6411
Fax: 207-777-6410

Maryland

Allfirst Bank

Allied Capital SBLC Corporation

Write Action Plan Notes

Amresco Independence Funding, Inc.

Bank of America, N.A.

Bank Annapolis

Branch Banking & Trust (BB&T)

Business Loan Center

Carrollton Bank

Massachusetts

Abington Savings Bank *

Mr. James Hanlon, Vice President
533 Washington St.
Abington, MA 02351
Tel: 781-982-3667
Fax: 781-878-4149

Bank of Western Massachusetts *

Mr. Steven Robinson, Vice President
29 State St.
Springfield, MA 01103
Tel: 413-781-2265
Fax: 413-781-8022

Bay State Savings Bank

Mr. Walter Dwyer, Vice President
28 Franklin St.
Worcester, MA 01608

Tel: 508-890-9051
Fax: 508-751-6459

Business Lenders, LLC

Ms. Nancy Reynolds, Vice President
49 Walnut Park Bldg. #5
Wellesley, MA 02481
Tel: 781-416-9993
Fax: 781-416-9995

Cape Cod Bank & Trust Co.

Ms. Berta Bruinooge, Assistant Vice President
307 Main St.
Hyannis, MA 02601
Tel: 508-862-6431
Fax: 508-760-9378

Capital Crossing Bank

Mr. Kenneth Weidman, Senior Vice President
101 Summer St.
Boston, MA 02110
Tel: 617-880-1000
Fax: 617-880-1010

Michigan

Business Loan Center

2250 Butterfield Drive, Suite 201
Troy, MI 48084
Tel: 248-273-2200

Write Action Plan Notes

CIT Small Business Lending Corp.

2843 East Grand River #148
East Lansing, MI 48823
Tel: 517-699-2331

Citizens Bank

328 S. Saginaw Street
Flint, MI 48502
Tel: 810-237-4907

First International Bank

12900 Hall Road, Suite 270
Sterling Heights, MI 48313
Tel: 586-323-1253

First Union Small Business Capital

42705 Grand River Avenue, Suite 201
Novi, MI 48375
Tel: 248-344-9573

Comerica Bank

3551 Hamlin Road
Auburn Hills, MI 48326-7355
Tel: 248-371-6070

Minnesota

1578 University Avenue

St. Paul MN 55104
Tel: 651-628-2661

1215 Pokegama Ave So
Grand Rapids MN 55744
Tel: 218-327-1121

14665 Galaxie Ave, Suite 350
Apple Valley MN 55124
Tel: 952-808-8075

1270 Yankee Doodle Road
Eagan MN 55121-2231
Tel: 651-306-1657

1083-3rd Street NW
Roseau MN 56751
Tel: 218-463-3888

11800 Aberdeen St, Suite 120
Blaine, MN 55449
Tel: 763-862-9962

8800 Highway 7
St Louis Park MN 55426
Tel: 952-932-6592

Mississippi

Community Bank—Desoto County

Contact: Clay Dunn, Senior Vice-President
P.O. Box 129
Southaven, Mississippi 38671
Tel: 662-280-9700
Fax: 662-349-4700

Write Action Plan Notes

First Security Bank

Contact: Jeff Herron, Vice President
P.O. Box 690
Batesville, Mississippi 38606
Tel: 662-563-9311
Fax: 662-563-9310

Hancock Bank

Contact: Tom Collins, Assistant Vice President
P.O. Box 4019
Gulfport, Mississippi 39501
Tel: 228-868-4000
Fax: 228-868-4675

Merchants & Farmers Bank

Contact: Ritchie Berry, Branch President
P.O. Box 520
Kosciusko, Mississippi 39090
Tel: 601-289-8511
Fax: 601-289-4801

National Bank of Commerce

Contact: Dan Craig, Vice-President
P.O. Box 1187
Starkville, Mississippi 39759
Tel: 662-323-1341
Fax: 662-324-4790

Missouri

Union Planters Bank, N.A.

407 N. Kingshighway
Cape Girardeau, MO 63701
Tel: 573-335-0893

CIT Small Business Lending Corporation

400 Chesterfield Center Dr., Suite 400
Chesterfield, MO 63017
Tel: 636-458-2330

U.S. Bank National Association

16402 Swingley Ridge Rd., Suite 340
Chesterfield, MO 63017
Tel: 636-778-0110

Commerce Bank

8000 Forsyth Boulevard
Clayton, MO 63105
Tel: 314-726-2255

Boone County National Bank

720 East Broadway
Columbia, MO 65201
Tel: 573-874-8100

Write Action Plan Notes

Montana

Yellowstone Bank

P.O. Box 10
Absarokee, MT 59001
Tel: 406-328-4512

United Bank,.A.

P.O. Box 480
Absarokee, MT 59001
Tel: 406-328-4742

Amsterdam-Churchill Bank

7175 Churchill Road
Amsterdam, MT 59741
Tel: 406-282-7175

Glacier Bank

307 East Park
Anaconda, MT 59711
Tel: 406-563-5203

First   National   Bank   of
Montana, Inc.

207 Main
Anaconda, MT 59711
Tel: 406-563-8303

Wells Fargo Bank Montana,.A.

120 West Park Avenue
Anaconda, MT 59711
Tel: 406-563-4146

Valley Bank

17925 Highway 93
Arlee, MT 59821
Tel: 406-726-2000

Nebraska

Adams Bank & Trust

315 North Spruce
Ogallala, NE 69153-2517
Tel: 308-284-4071
Fax: 308-284-3207

Bank of Nebraska

7223 So. 84th St.
LaVista, NE 68128-2130
Tel: 402-331-8550
Fax: 402-331-8570

First National Bank of North
Platte

201 North Dewey St.
North Platte, NE 68101-4036
Tel: 308-532-1000
Fax: 308-535-6289

Five Points Bank

2015 North Broadwell Ave.
Grand Island, NE 68803-2759
Tel: 308-384-5350
Fax: 308-384-9783

Write Action Plan Notes

Heritage Bank

1333 No. Webb Rd.
Grand Island, NE 68803
Tel: 308-384-5538
Fax: 308-384-6778

Nevada

American Bank of Commerce

Bank of America Nevada

First Interstate Bank of Nevada, N.A.

First Security Bank of Nevada

Kirkwood Bank and Trust Co. dba Kirkwood Lending Center

Nevada State Bank

U.S. Bank of Nevada

New Hampshire

Bank of New Hampshire

BayBank NH, N.A.

The Berlin City Bank

Centerpoint Bank

CFX Bank

Citizens Bank New Hampshire

Concord Savings Bank

First Essex Bank, FSB

Fleet Bank-NH

Granite Bank

KeyBank National Association

NH Business Dev. Corp.

Primary Bank

New Jersey

Washington Mutual Bank, FA

Contact: Ms. Donna Haibeck,
Vice President
17 Lancelot Lane
Basking Ridge, NJ 07920
Tel: 908-696-9611
Fax: 908-696-9612

Fleet Bank

Contact: Ms. Lucia DiNapoli
Gibbons, Executive Vice
President
Regional Director Small
Business Services NJ/PA
1125 Route 22 West
Bridgewater, NJ 08807
Tel: 908-253-4020
Fax: 908-253-4130

Write Action Plan Notes

Commerce Bank/Shore, N.A.

Contact: Renae   Jordan,
Assistant Vice President
SBA Lending
1701 Route 70 East
Tel: 732-505-3000 Ext.2515
Fax: 732-505-2907

G.E. Capital Small Business
Fin. Corp.

Contact: Mr. Larry Sherman,
Business   Development
Executive
100 Walnut Avenue, 6th Floor
Clark, NJ 07066-1247
Tel: 732-388-3188
Fax: 732-815-3192

Unity Bank

Contact: Mr. Michael Downs,
Sr Vice Pres & SBA Manager
64 Old Highway 22
Clinton, NJ 08809
Tel: 908-730-7630
Fax: 908-713-4391

New Mexico

Bank of America, FSB

201 3rd St NW
Albuquerque, NM 87102
Tel: 1-800-263-2055

Charter Bank for Savings FSB

4400 Osuna Rd NE
Albuquerque, NM 87109
Tel: 505-341-7300

Compass Bank

505 Marquette NW
Albuquerque, NM 87102
Tel: 505-888-9020

InterAmerica Bank

2400 Louisiana Blvd NE
Albuquerque, NM 87110
Tel: 505-880-1700

Sunrise Bank of Albuquerque

225 Gold SW
Albuquerque, NM 87102
Tel: 505-244-8000

Wells Fargo Bank New Mexico, NA

200 Lomas NW
Albuquerque, NM 87002
Tel: 505-766-6423

New York

Manufactures & Traders Trust
Co.

New York Business Development
Corporation

M & T Bank

Write Action Plan Notes

HSBC Bank USA

Chase Manhattan

Citibank

Key Bank

North Carolina

Branch Banking & Trust Company (BB&T)

Business Loan Center, LLC

California Bank & Trust

Capital Bank

Capital One Federal Savings Bank

Central Carolina Bank & Trust Company

CIT Small Business Lending Corp.

Comerica Bank

The East Carolina Bank

The Fidelity Bank

First Citizens Bank & Trust Co.

North Dakota

Bank Center First (SBA Express)

320 North Fourth Street
Bismarck, ND 58501
Tel: 701-258-2611

BNC National Bank

322 East Main
Bismarck, ND 58502
Tel: 701-250-3000

Kirkwood Bank and Trust Co.

Seventh Street & Arbor Avenue
Bismarck, ND 58506
Tel: 701-258-6550

Bremer Bank, N.A.

424 Fifth Street
Devils Lake, ND 58301
Tel: 701-662-4074

American State Bank & Trust

140 First Avenue West
Dickinson, ND 58601
Tel: 701-225-6811

Write Action Plan Notes

Ohio

FirstMerit Bank, NA

106 South Main Street
Akron OH 44308
Contact: Thomas C. Lundberg
Tel: 330-384-7399
Fax: 330-996-8003

Bank One

8044 Montgomery Road
Cincinnati OH 45202
Contact: Larry Bradley
Tel: 513-985-5569
Fax: 513-985-5060

Citi Capital Small Business
Finance

1232 W. Kemper Rd. #282
Cincinnati OH 45240
Contact: Rick Dees
Tel: 513-729-5200
Fax: 513-729-5222

Fifth   Third   Bank   of
Cincinnati

38 Fountain Square Plaza—MD
10905D
Cincinnati OH 45263
Contact: Michael Shepherd
Tel: 513-534-8188
Fax: 513-579-5226

Firstar Bank

425 Walnut Street

Cincinnati OH 45202
Contact: Robin Nenninger
Tel: 513-632-2370
Fax: 513-632-2388

Oklahoma

Albright   Title   &   Trust
Company+

P.O. Box 51
Newkirk, OK 74647-0051
Contact: John Birch, Senior
Vice President
Tel: 580-362-2525

Americrest Bank+

P.O. Box 25676
Oklahoma   City,   OK   73125-
0676
Contact: Tracy Renfro, Vice
President
Tel: 405-951-9019

BancFirst*+

101 N. Broadway, Suite 460
Oklahoma   City,   OK   73102-
8405
Contact: Kent   Faison,
President
Tel: 405-270-4736

Bank of America, N.A.*+

10343 E. 71 St.
Tulsa, OK 74133

Write Action Plan Notes

Contact: Sam Vaverka, Govt. Lending Spec
Tel: 918-307-8281

Bank of Oklahoma, N.A.*+

7701 S. Western
Oklahoma City, OK 73139-2400
Contact: Kevin Guarnera, Senior Vice President
Tel: 405-616-7501

Oregon

Albina Community Bank

2002 NE MLK, Jr. Blvd
Portland, OR 97212
Contact: Mike Lauinger, SVP
Tel: 503-331-3782
Fax: 503-287-0197
Email: mlauinger@albinabank.com

Bank of America, NA

10555 NE 8th Street
Bellevue, WA 98006
Contact: Patricia Rogers, SBA Loan Specialist
Tel: 206-358-5146
Fax: 206-585-5411
Email: patricia.l.rogers@bankofamerica.com

Bank of Astoria (SBA Express)

1122 Duane Street
PO Box 28
Astoria, OR 97103
Contact: Rhonda Wills, SVP
Tel: 503-325-8486 Ext. 32
Fax: 503-325-8487 or 325-6332
Email: rwills@bankofastoria.com

Bank of the Cascades

1100 NW Wall Street
Bend, OR 97701
Contact: Cathie Hendrix, AVP & Bus. Loan Officer
Tel: 541-617-3616
Fax: 541-617-3617
Email: cathieh@botc.com

Bank of Clark County

PO Box 61725
Vancouver, WA 98666-1725
Contact: Darryl M. Horowitz, AVP
Tel: 360-906-9514
Fax: 360-694-7164
Email: darrylh@bankclark-county.com

Philadelphia

Business Loan Express

100 Springhouse Dr
Suite 105
Collegeville, PA 19426
Contact: Greg Poehlman, Vice President
Tel: 610-831-9080 Ext. 11

Write Action Plan Notes

Citizens Bank of PA

2001 Market Street
Suite 600
Philadelphia, PA 19103
Contact: Len Prevo, Vice
President
Tel: 267-671-1026

CIT Small Business

Lending Corp.
634 York Rd
PMB 167
Warminster, PA 18974
Contact: Frank Gallagher,
Regional Account Manager
Tel: 215-918-2542

Commerce Bank/Harrisburg, N.A.

100 Senate Avenue
Camp Hill, PA 17011
Contact: Brian Weikert,
Director SBA Programs
Tel: 717-243-4793

Commerce Bank/PA, N.A.

Glenview Corp Ctr.
Suite 407
3220 Tillman Drive
Bensalem, PA 19020
Contact: Rose Voltz
Tel: 215-604-6239

Eagle National Bank

8045 West Chester Pike

Upper Darby, PA 19082
Contact: Grant Conway,
Senior Vice President
Tel: 610-853-4800 Ext. 1234

Rhode Island

Bank of Newport

500 West Main Road
Middletown, RI, 02842
Contact: Joseph Lavin, Vice
President
Tel: 401-845-8726

Bank RI*

One Turks Head Place
Providence, RI, 02903
Contact: David Goolgasian,
Vice President
Tel: 401-456-5015 Ext. 1998

Citizens Bank*

One Citizens Plaza
Providence, RI, 02903
Contact: Judith Cadigan-
Parisi, Vice President
Tel: 401-456-7324
Gary Heidel, Director,
Government Guaranty Programs
Tel: 401-734-5617

Coastway Credit Union*

10 Greene Street
Providence, RI, 02903

Write Action Plan Notes

Contact: Russell   Gaston,
Commercial Lending Manager
Tel: 401-455-3200

Domestic Bank

815 Reservoir Avenue
Cranston, RI, 02910
Contact: H. Jeffrey Baker,
Vice President
Tel: 401-943-1600

South Carolina

Temecula Valley Bank

5 Terrapin Trail
Taylors, SC 29687
Tel: 864-268-4912
Fax: 864-268-7631

South Carolina Bank & Trust

520 Gervais St.
Columbia, SC 29202
Tel: 803-231-3361
Fax: 803-771-0615

Goleta National Bank

26 Office Park Court, Suite
102
Columbia, SC 29223
Tel: 803-736-1804
Fax: 803-736-6994

Lighthouse Community Bank

P.O. Box 5697
Greenville, SC 29606
Tel: 864-232-5080
Fax: 864-232-2444

First National Bank

P.O. Box 1287
Orangeburg, SC 29115
Tel: 803-531-0522
Fax: 803-531-8757

South Dakota

First   National   Bank   in
Brookings

PO Drawer 5057
Belle Fourche, SD
Tel: 605-696-2200

First Fidelity Bank

PO Box 376
Burke, SD
Tel: 605-775-2641

The First Western Bank

648 Mt. Rushmore Rd.
Custer
Tel: 605-673-2215

First National Bank

PO Box 850
Ft. Pierre
Tel: 605-223-2521

Write Action Plan Notes

American State Bank

PO Box 1178
Pierre
Tel: 605-224-9233

Tennessee

Citizens Bank

300 Broad Street
Elizabethton, TN 37643
Tel: 423-543-2265
Fax: 423-547-8424

Tennessee Business and
Industrial Dev. Corp.

P.O. Box 307
Paris, TN 38242
Tel: 731-644-7108
Fax: 731-644-7019

Bank of Murfreesboro

615 Memorial Blvd.
Murfreesboro, TN 37129
Tel: 615-890-1111
Fax: 615-890-1905

Capital Bank & Trust Co.

1820 W. End Avenue
Nashville, TN 37202
Tel: 615-327-9000
Fax: 615-321-2126

Citizens National Bank

2 Park Avenue
Athens, TN 37371
Tel: 423-745-0261
Fax: 423-745-7718

First Federal Savings Bank

200 N. Second Street
Clarksville, TN 37041
Tel: 931-552-6176
Fax: 931-552-7763

Texas

Northwest National Bank of
Arlington

Zion Small Business Finance

Arlington National Bank

Citizens National Bank

First National Bank of Texas

First State Bank of North
Texas

Abrams Centre National Bank

AMRESCO Independence Funding

Banco Popular, N.A. (Texas)

Bank of America N.A.

Write Action Plan Notes

Utah

American Bank of Commerce

3670 N. University Ave
Provo, UT 84604
Tel: 801-377-4222

America First Credit Union.

4646 S. 1500 W
Riverdale, UT 84405
Tel: 801-778-8604

American Investment Financial

525 E. South Temple
Salt Lake City, UT 84102
Tel: 801-521-1078

Bank of America, FSB

6900 Westcliff Drive, 3rd
Floor
Las Vegas, NV 89128
Tel: 801-531-1476

Bank of American Fork

33 E. Main
American Fork, UT 84003
Tel: 801-756-7681

Bank of Commerce

330 N. Brand Blvd., Ste 1285
Glendale, CA 91203
Tel: 818-548-7400

Vermont

Banknorth

111 Main Street
P.O. Box 409
Burlington, VT 05401
Tel: 802-658-1010
Fax: 802-860-5542

KeyBank, N.A.

149 Bank Street
P.O. Box 949
Burlington, VT 05402
Tel: 802-660-4293
Fax: 802-864-6908

Lyndonville Savings Bank
98 Broad Street
Lyndonville, VT 05851
Tel: 802-626-1111
Fax: 802-626-3456

Factory Point National Bank

Equinox Square
P.O. Box 1566
Manchester Center, VT 05255
Tel: 802-362-2424
Fax: 802-362-4101

National Bank of Middlebury

22-32 Main Street
P.O. Box 189
Middlebury, VT 05753
Tel: 802-388-4982
Fax: 802-388-6077

Write Action Plan Notes

Virginia

Bank of America

1111 East Main Street, 8th Floor
VA2-300-08-02
Richmond, VA 23219
Contact: Paulita Biddle, Assistant Vice President
Tel: 804-788-2775
Fax: 804-788-3569

Bank of Northumberland, Inc.

14953 Northumberland Highway
Burgess, VA 22432
Contact: Reuben Thrift, Vice President
Tel: 804-453-7003
Fax: 804-453-6242

Branch, Banking & Trust Company (BB&T)

5901-C Peachtree Dunwoody Road
Suite 420
Atlanta, GA 30328
Contact: Travis York
Loan Officer
Tel: 770-522-0789
Fax: 770-551-8781

Business Lenders, LLC

15 Lewis Street
Hartford, CT 06103
Contact: Penn Ritter, President and CEO

Tel: 860-244-9202
Fax: 860-527-0884

Business Loan Express

3 South 12th Street
Richmond, VA 23219
Contact: Deborah C. Hudson, Senior Vice President
Tel: 804-344-8160 or 1-888-333-6441
Fax: 804-344-8301

Washington

American Marine Bank

P.O. Box 10788
Bainbridge Island, WA 98110
Tel: 206-842-5651

Anchor Savings Bank

120 N. Broadway
P.O. Box 387
Aberdeen, WA 98520-0094
Tel: 360-532-6222

Bank Northwest

100 Grand Avenue
Bellingham, WA 98225
Tel: 360-734-0544

Charter Bank

320 108th Avenue
Bellevue, WA 98004-5734
Tel: 425-586-5020

Write Action Plan Notes

Comerica Bank PLP

500 108th Avenue NE, 16th
Floor
Bellevue, WA 98004
Tel: 425-454-9294

West Virginia

WesBanco

1 Bank Plaza
Wheeling, WV 26003
Contact: Jim Croft
Tel: 304-234-9291

Bank One West Virginia

1000 Fifth Avenue
PO Box 179
Huntington, WV 25706
Contact: David Graley, Vice
President
Tel: 304-526-4333

Bank One West Virginia

755 East Stratton Street
Logan, WV 25601
Contact: Rory Perry,
President
Tel: 304-752-1023

Bank One West Virginia

500 Neville Street
Beckley, WV 25801

Contact: Nancy Kissinger,
President
Tel: 304-256-2157

Bank One West Virginia

707 Virginia Street East
Charleston, WV 25301
Contact: Ronald Beane,
President
Tel: 304-348-6948

Wisconsin

Bank Mutual, Milwaukee, WI

Website: www.bankmutual.com
Contact: Joseph Martin,
Vice President
Tel: 414-371-8272
Fax: 414-371-8230

American National Bank-Fox
Cities, Appleton, WI

Website:
http://americannationalbank.org
Contact: David Blohm,
President or Lon Rupnow,
Vice President
Tel: 920-739-1040
Fax: 920-739-9216

Associated Bank, N.A.,
Green Bay, WI

Website:
www.associatedbank.com

Write Action Plan Notes

Contact: Joseph W. Fikejs, Assistant Vice President- SBA Program Manager
Tel: 920-727-8383
Fax: 920-727-5367

Bank Mutual, Milwaukee, WI

Website: www.bankmutual.com
Contact: Joseph Martin, Vice President
Tel: 414-371-8272
Fax: 414-371-8230

Bank One Wisconsin

Website: www.bankone.com
SBA Lending
Tel: 888-536-3722

Wyoming

First Interstate Bank

P.O. Box 2007
Sheridan, WY 82801
Contact: Ed Garding, President
Tel: 307-674-7411

First National Bank of Gillette

Box 3002
Gillette, WY 82717
Contact: Don R. Johnson, Senior Vice President
Tel: 307-682-9308

First National Bank of Laramie

P.O. Box 490
Laramie, WY 82070
Contact: Dan Furphy, President
Tel: 307-742-4625

The Jackson State Bank

P.O. Box 1788
Jackson, WY 83001
Contact: Peter Lawton, Senior Vice-President
Tel: 307-733-3737

First National Bank and Trust Co.

P.O. Box 907
Powell, WY 82435
Contact: Bob Nemitz, Vice President
Tel: 307-754-2201
Fax: 307-754-1414

Puerto Rico

Citibank

P.O. Box 364106
San Juan, PR 00936-4106
Contact: Brunilda De Rivera
Tel: 787-766-3611
Fax: 787-766-3610

Write Action Plan Notes

Banco Bilbao Vizacaya of Puerto Rico

P.O. Box 364745
San Juan, PR 00936-4745
Contact: Arturo Villanueva, VP
Tel: 787-777-2889
Fax: 787-766-6985

Banco Popular de Puerto Rico
P.O. Box 362708

San Juan, PR 00936-2708
Contact: Mary Carmen Ochoa
Tel: 787-765-9800
Fax: 787-756-5055

Banco Santander Puerto Rico
P.O. Box 362589

San Juan, PR 00936-2589
Contact: Antonio O'neill, VP
Tel: 787-759-7070
Fax: 787-765-7443

Firstbank

P.O. Box 9146
San Juan, PR 00908-9146
Contact: Migdalia Rivera
Tel: 787-729-8037
Fax: 787-729-8153

Write Action Plan Notes

MicroLoan Lenders by State

1   ALABAMA

MICROLOAN PROGRAMS IN ALABAMA

The MicroLoan Program provides small loans ranging from as little as $100 to $35,000. Under this program, the SBA makes funds available to nonprofit intermediaries; these, in turn, make the loans. Interest rates vary, depending upon the intermediary lender. Rates are generally competitive. This program is available at a limited number of locations.

USE OF PROCEEDS—Microloans may be used to finance furniture, machinery, equipment, fixtures, inventory, and/or working capital.

There are three intermediary lenders in the State of Alabama:

1   Birmingham Business Resource Center

    110 12th Street North
    Birmingham, AL 35203
    Executive Director: Robert Dickerson, Jr.
    E-mail: bbrc@inlinenet.net
    Website: www.bbrconline.com
    Tel: (205)250-6380 Fax (205)250-6384
    Service Area: Jefferson County.

2   Community Enterprise Investments, Inc.

    302 North Barcelona Street
    Pensacola, FL 32501
    Executive Director: Daniel Horvath
    Microloan Contact: Richard Jemison
    E-mail: rjemison@ceii-cdc.org
            bigdanfla@aol.com

Write Action Plan Notes

eljojr@aol.com

ceii2234@aol.com

Website: www.ceii.pensacola.com

Tel: (850) 595-6234   Fax (850) 595-6264

Toll Free: 1-888-605-2505

Service Area: Autauga, Baldwin, Barbour, Butler, Bullock, Choctaw, Clarke, Coffee, Conecuh, Covington, Crenshaw, Dale, Dallas, Escambia, Geneva, Greene, Henry, Houston, Lee, Lowndes, Marengo, Mobile, Monroe, Montgomery, Perry, Pike, Russell, Sumter, Washington and Wilcox counties.

3   Southeast Community Capital

1020 Commerce Park Drive, Suite L5

Oak Ridge, TN 37830

Executive Director: Clint Gwin

Microloan Contact: Allen Summery

                  Clint Gwin

                  David Bradshaw

E-mail: gwin@sccapital.org

Website: www.tech2020.org

Tel: Clint Gwin-(615) 473-2445,

Allen Summery-(423) 425-3774,

David Bradshaw-(865) 220-2025.

Fax: (865) 220-2024

Service Area: Bibb, Blount, Calhoun, Chambers, Cherokee, Chilton, Clay, Cleburne, Colbert, Coosa, Cullman, DeKalb, Elmore, Etowah, Fayette, Franklin, Hale, Jackson, Jefferson, Lamar, Lauderdale, Lawrence, Limestone, Macon, Madison, Marion, Marshall, Morgan, Pickens, Randolph, St. Clair, Shelby, Talladega, Tallapoosa, Tuscaloosa, Walker and Winston counties.

Lender policy does not allow for loans less than $10,000 nor for restaurants.

2   **ARIZONA**

MICROLOAN LENDER PARTICIPANTS—PHOENIX, ARIZONA

Arizona District Office—MICROLOAN PROGRAM

Write Action Plan Notes

Participating Microloan Lenders and Technical Assistance Providers

1   Arizona Council for Economic Conversion (ACEC)

10 East Broadway, Suite 210
P.O. Box 42108
Tucson, Arizona 85733
Tel: 520.620.1241 FAX: 520.622.2235
Web site: http://www.acec-az.org
Service Area: Pima County.

2   Chicanos Por La Causa, Inc.

1107 E. Tonto Street, Suite B103
Phoenix, Arizona 85034
Tel: 602.252.0483 FAX: 602.252.0484
Web site: http://www.cplc.org
Service Area: Urban Maricopa and Pima counties, Graham and Gila counties (including Point of Pines Reservation and the Southwestern area of Fort Apache Reservation), Coconino and Mohave Counties (including the Kaibab, Havasupai, and Hualapai Reservations and western portions of the Navajo and Hopi Reservations), Yavapai and La Paz Counties.

3   PPEP Microbusiness and Housing Development Corporation, Inc.

901 East 46th Street
Tucson, Arizona 85713
Tel: 520.622.3553 FAX 520.622.1480
Web site: www.azsmallbusinessloans.com
Service Area: Cochise, Santa Cruz, Pinal, Yuma, rural Pima, and rural Maricopa counties including the Fort Mcdowell, Gila River, Maricopa, Papago, Salt River, and San Xavier Indian Reservations.

Write Action Plan Notes

4   Self Employment Loan Fund (SELF)

201 North Central Avenue, Suite CC100
Phoenix, AZ 85073
Tel: 602.340.8834 FAX 602.340.8953
Web site: www.selfloanfund.org
Service Area: Maricopa County
Maximum Loan Amount: $15,000.00

3   ARKANSAS

MICROLOAN Lenders—ARKANSAS

Intermediary Lenders

1   Arkansas Enterprise Group

605 Main Street, Suite 203
Arkadelphia, Arkansas 71923
Tel: (870) 246-9739
Service Area: Southern and extreme northeast areas of
the State including Arkansas, Ashley, Bradley,
Calhoun, Chicot, Clark, Clay, Cleveland, Columbia,
Craighead, Dallas, Desha, Drew, Garland, Grant,
Greene, Hempstead, Hot Spring, Howard, Jefferson
Lafayette, Lawrence, Lincoln, Little River, Lonoke,
Miller, Mississippi, Montgomery, Nevada, Ouachita,
Phillips, Pike, Poinsett, Polk, Prairie, Pulaski,
Randolph, Saline, Sevier, and Union Counties.

2   Delta Community Development Corp.

335 Broadway/P.O.B. 852, Forrest City, AR 72336
Executive Director: Willtte Romous
Microloan Contact: Pat Scott
E-mail: deltacdc@ipa.net
Tel: (870) 633-9112. Fax: (870) 633-9191
Service Area: East Arkansas—Cross, Crittenden, Lee,
Monroe, and St. Francis counties.

Write Action Plan Notes

3   FORGE, Inc.

P.O. Box 1138
Huntsville, Arkansas 72740
Tel: (501) 738-1585
Service Area: Northwest Arkansas—Crawford, Baxter,
Yell, Perry, Conway, Boone, Madison,
Marion, Carroll, Franklin, Pope, Benton, Washington,
Searcy, and Newton.

4   Good Faith Fund (affiliate of AEG)

2304 W 29th St.
Pine Bluff, Arkansas 71603
Tel: (870) 535-6233
Area served: Ashley, Bradley, Chicot, Cleveland,
Desha, Drew, Jefferson and Lincoln counties.

5   White River Planning and Development District, Inc.

1625 White Drive
Batesville, Arkansas 72503
Tel: (870) 793-5233

Service Area: North Central Arkansas—Cleburne, Fulton,
Independence, Izard, Jackson, Sharp, Stone, Van Buren,
White, and Woodruff counties.

4   COLORADO

MICROLOAN DEMONSTRATION PROGRAM—COLORADO

Participating Intermediary Lenders and
Non-Lending Technical Assistance Providers

Intermediary Lenders Colorado

1   Colorado Enterprise Fund

1888 Sherman St, Suite 530

Write Action Plan Notes

Denver, CO 80203
Contact: Lewis Hagler
Tel: (303) 860-0242. Fax: (303) 860-0409
Web page: www.coloradoenterprisefund.org
e-mail: microloans@coloradoenterprisefund.org
Service Area: City and County of Denver, Adams,
Arapahoe,
Boulder, Douglas, Jefferson, Larimer, Weld, Elbert
and El Paso counties.

2   Colorado Region 10 LEAP, Inc.

P.O. Box 849, Montrose, CO 81402
300 North Cascade Street, Suite 1
Montrose, CO 81401
Contact: Jonathan Allen
Telephone: (970) 249-2436. Fax: 970) 249-2488
Service Area: West Central area including Delta,
Gunnison,
Hinsdale, Montrose, Ouray, and San Miguel counties.

5   CALIFORNIA

MICROLOAN DEMONSTRATION PROGRAM—CALIFORNIA

Participating Intermediary Lenders and
Non-Lending Technical Assistance Providers

Intermediary Lenders

1   Arcata Economic Development Corporation (AEDC)

100 Ericson Court, Suite 100A, Arcata, CA 95521
kellid@aedc1.org
Tel: (707) 822-4616. Fax: (707) 822-8982
Service Area: Del Norte, Humboldt, Lake, Mendocino,
Siskiyou, and Trinity counties.

Write Action Plan Notes

2   California Coastal Rural Development Corporation

221 Main St., Suite 300, Salinas, CA 93901
Mailing Address: P.O. Box 479, Salinas, CA 93902
Executive Director: Herb Aarons
Microloan Contact: Wendy Dodson
E-mail: wendy_dodson@calcoastal.org
Tel: (831) 424-1099. Fax: (831) 424-1094
Service Area: Santa Clara, Santa Cruz, Monterey, San
Benito, San Luis Obispo, Santa Barbara, Ventura coun-
ties.

3   California Coastal Rural Development Corp.

39 East De La Guerra Street, Santa Barbara, CA 93101
Tel: (805)962-9251
Service Area: Ventura and Santa Barbara Counties.

4   FAME Renaissance Center

1968 West Adams Boulevard, Los Angeles, CA 90018
Tel: (323)730-7700, ext. 530
Service Area: Los Angeles and Ventura Counties.

5   Pacific Coast Regional Small Business Development
Corporation

3255 Wilshire Boulevard, Suite 1501, Los Angeles, CA
90010
Tel: (213)739-2999, ext. 222
Service Area: Los Angeles County California.

6   Southeast Asian Community Center

875 O'Farrell Street, San Francisco, CA 94109
Tel: (415) 885-2743. Fax: (415) 885-3253
Service Area: Alameda, Contra Costa, Marin, Merced,
Sacramento, San Francisco, San Joaquin, San Mateo,
Santa Clara, and Stanislaus counties.

Write Action Plan Notes

7   Valley Economic Development Corporation

5121 Van Nuys Blvd. 3rd Floor, Van Nuys, CA 91403
E-mail: roberto@vedc.org
Tel: (818) 907-9977. Fax: (818) 907-9720
Service Area: Los Angeles and Orange County.

6   CONNECTICUT

CONNECTICUT DISTRICT OFFICE

Intermediary Lenders:

1   Connecticut Community Investment Corporation

100 Crown Street, New Haven, CT 06510
Contact: John Torello, Loan Officer
E-Mail: JTorello@ctcic.org
Contact: Gary Toole, Loan Officer
E-Mail: GToole@ctcic.org
Tel: (203) 776-6172. Fax: (203) 776-6837
Service Area: Nationwide.

2   Community Economic Development Fund

50-G Weston Street, Hartford, CT 06120
Contact: Donna Wertenbach, President
E-Mail: D.Wertenbach@cedf.com
Tel: (860) 249-3800 ext. 308 OR (800) 656-4613.
Fax: (860) 249-2500
Service Area: Nationwide.

7   DISTRICT OF COLUMBIA

MICROLOAN DEMONSTRATION PROGRAM—DISTRICT OF COLUMBIA

Write Action Plan Notes

Intermediary Lenders

1   ARCH Development Corporation

1227 Good Hope Road, SE, Washington, DC 20020
Executive Director: Duane Gautier
Microloan Contact: Teina Linthicum (202) 678-7856
E-Mail:
Tel: (202) 889-5023. Fax: (202) 889-5035
Service Area: Portions of the District of Columbia
commonly referred to as Adams Morgan, Mount Pleasant
and Anacostia, Congress Heights, Columbia Heights,
and 14th Street Corridor.

2   H Street Community Development Corporation

501 H Street, NE, Washington, DC 20002
Executive Director: William Barrow
Microloan Contact: Yulonda Queen
E-mail: oomhscdc@aol.com
Tel: (202) 544-8353. Fax: (202) 544-3051
Service Area: West-the Anacostia River; East-7th
Street, N.W.;
North-Benning Road to K Street; and South-the
Southeast/Southwest Freeway: Servicing Capitol Hill,
H Street-N.E., Lincoln Park, Mt. Vernon Square,
Judiciary Square, Benning Road-West of the Anacostia
River, Union Station, Stadium Armory, and Lower North
Capitol.

8   DELAWARE

MICROLOAN DEMONSTRATION PROGRAM—DELAWARE

Intermediary Lenders

1   Wilmington Economic Development Corporaton

100 W. 10th St., Suite 706, Wilmington, DE 19801
Executive Director: Constance McCarthy

Write Action Plan Notes

Microloan Contact: Constance McCarthy
E-mail: wedco@wedcode.org
Tel: (302) 571-9088. Fax: (302) 652-5679
Service Area: New Castle county, in the cities of Wilmington, Newark, New Castle, Middletown, Odessa, and Townsend.

9   FLORIDA

MICROLOAN PROGRAM—FLORIDA

Participating Intermediary Lenders

1   Community Equity Investments, Inc.

302 North Barcelona Street, Pensacola, FL 32501
Executive Director: Dan Horvath
Microloan Contact: Elbert Jones
E-mail: bigdanfla@aol.com
Tel: 850-595-6234. Fax: 850-595-6264
Service Area: Florida Panhandle including Bay, Calhoun, Escambia, Gadsden, Gulf, Jackson, Holmes, Liberty, Leon, Franklin, Wakulla,Walton, Washington, Okaloosa, and Santa Rosa counties.

2   Clearwater Neighborhood Housing Services, Inc.

608 North Garden Avenue
Clearwater, Florida 33755
Executive Director: Isay M. Gulley
Microloan Contact: John Moloney
E-mail: igulley@hotmail.com
Tel: 727-442-4155. Fax: 727-446-4911
Service Area: City of Clearwater and Pinellas county Florida.

3   Minority/Women Business Enterprise Alliance, Inc.

3700 43th Street, Suite 100
Orlando, Florida 32805

Write Action Plan Notes

Executive Director: Geovanny Sepulveda
Microloan Contact: Geovanny Sepulveda
E-mail: alliabiz@bellsouth.net
Telephone: 407-428-5860. Fax: 407-428-5869
Service Area: Brevard, Lake, Marion, Orange, Osceola, Polk, Seminole, Sumter and Volusia Counties.

4   The Business Loan Fund of the Palm Beaches, Inc.

324 Datura Street, Suite 201
West Palm Beach, Florida 33401
Executive Director: John B. Brown
Microloan Contact: John B. Brown
E-mail: blfpb@evcom.net
Telephone: 561-838-9027. Fax: 561-838-9029
Service Area: Hendry, Indian River, Martin, Palm Beach and St. Lucie Counties.

5   United Gainesville Community Dev. Corp., Inc.

505 NW 2nd Avenue
P.O.B. 2518, Gainesville, FL 32602
Interim Executive Director: Appie L. Graham
E-mail: info@ugcdc.org
Telephone: 352-334-0943. Fax: 352-334-0947
Service Area: Alachua, and Marion counties Florida.

6   Micro Business USA (a.k.a Working Capital Florida)

3000 Biscayne Boulevard, Suite 102
Miami, Florida 33137
Executive Director: Diane Silverman
Microloan Contact: Diane Silverman
E-mail: Workcap@bellsouth.net
Tel: 305-438-1407 Ext. 400. Fax: 305-438-1411
Service Area: Broward, Miami-Dade, Palm Beach and Pinellas Counties.

Write Action Plan Notes

7   Central Florida Community Development Company

     P.O. Box 15065
     Daytona Beach, FL 32115
     Executive Director:
     Microloan Contact: Gerald Chester
     Telephone: 386-258-7520. Fax: 386-238-3428
     Service Area: Brevard County.

10   GEORGIA

     Georgia District Office Mission Statement~
     "To Provide Leadership for the Economic Growth
     of Georgia Communities Through the Development
     and Support of Small Business"

MicroLoan Lenders

1   ALBANY COMMUNITY TOGETHER, INC. (ACT!)

     230 S. Jackson Street, Suite 154
     Albany, Georgia 31701
     Microloan Contact: Thelma Adams Johnson
     Tel: 229/420-4600. Fax: 229/420-8311

2   DEKALB ENTERPRISE BUSINESS CORPORATION (DEBCO)

     750 Commerce Drive, Suite 201
     Decatur, Georgia 30030
     Microloan Contact: Charles Blackmon
     Tel: 404/378-1899. Fax: 404/377-3397

3   GRASP ENTERPRISE FUNDING CORPORATION

     241 Peachtree Street, NW-Suite 2000
     Atlanta, GA 30303
     Microloan Contact: Timothy Scott
     Tel: 404/659-5955. Fax: 404/880-9561

Write Action Plan Notes

4   SMALL BUSINESS ASSISTANCE CORPORATION

     111 E. Liberty Street, Ste 100
     Savannah, GA 31401
     Microloan Contact: Tony O'Reilly
     Phone: 912/232-4700. Fax: 912/232-0385

5   SOUTHEAST COMMUNITY CAPITAL CORPORATION

     f/k/a TECH 2020 FINANCE CORP.
     1020 Commerce Park Dr.
     Oak Ridge, TN. 37830
     Microloan Contact: David Bradshaw
     Telephone: 865/220-2025. Fax: 865/220-2024

11 GUAM

MICROLOAN DEMONSTRATION PROGRAM—GUAM 9/2002

Intermediary Lenders

1   Commonwealth Development Authority

     (Commonwealth of the Northern Mariana Islands)
     P.O. Box 2149
     Saipan MP 96950
     Contact: MaryLou S. Ada, Executive Director
     Phone: (670) 234-7145/7146/6293
     Fax: (670) 234-7144

12 HAWAII

MICROLOAN PROGRAM—HAWAII

Intermediary Lenders

1   Pacific Gateway Center

     720 North King Street, Honolulu, HI 96817

Write Action Plan Notes

Executive Director: Tin Myaing Thein
E-mail: myaing@aol.com/pgccynthia@hotmail.com
Tel: (808) 845-3918. Fax: (808) 842-1962
Service Area: Nationwide.

13 IOWA

MICROLOAN DEMONSTRATION PROGRAM—IOWA

Intermediary Lenders

Iowa Siouxland Economic Development Corporation

428 Insurance Center 507 7th St.
P.O. Box 447, Sioux City, IA 51102
Executive Director: Ken Beekley
Microloan Contact: Glenda Castleberry
E-mail: ken@simpco.org
Tel: (712) 279-6286. Fax: (712) 279-6920
Service Area: Cherokee, Ida, Monona, Plymouth, Sioux,
and Woodbury counties.

14 IDAHO

MICROLOAN DEMONSTRATION PROGRAM—IDAHO

Intermediary Lenders

1   Sage Community Resources

10624 W. Executive Drive, Boise, Idaho 83713
Executive Director: Kathleen Simko
Microloan Contact: Bob Richards
Web Page: http://www.sageidaho.com/
Tel: (208) 322-7033
Service Area: Payette, Washington, Adams, Valley,
Gem, Boise, Elmore, Ada, Canyon and Owhyee counties.

Write Action Plan Notes

2   Panhandle Area Council

11100 Airport Drive, Hayden, ID 83835-9743
Execuive Director: James Deffenbaugh
Microloan Contact Kay Kitchel
Web Page: http://www.pacni.org
Tel: (208) 772-0584
Service Area: Northern Panhandle including Benewah,
Bonner,
Boundary, Kotenai, and Shoshone Counties.

15 Illinois

MICROLOAN DEMONSTRATION PROGRAM—Illinois

Intermediary Lenders

1   Accion Chicago, Inc.

3245 W. 26th
Chicago, IL 60623
President: F. Leroy Pacheco
Microloan Contact: Jonathan Brereton
E-mail:lpacheco@accionchicago.org
Tel: 773-376-9004. Fax: 773-376-9048
Service Area: Cook County (including parts of
Chicago),
Lake, McHenry, Dekalb, Kane, Dupage, Kendall, Grundy,
Kankakee, Will, and Lasalle counties.

2   Justine Petersen Housing & Reinvestment Corporation

5031 Northrup Avenue
St. Louis, MO 63110
Executive Director: Robert Boyle
Microloan Contact: Sheri Fannigan-Vasquez
E-mail:sflanigan@justinepetersen.org
Tel: 314-664-5051 Ext. 117 Fax: 314-644-5364

Write Action Plan Notes

16 INDIANA

Intermediary Lenders

1 SEEDCOe

216 W. Allen Street
Bloomington, IN 47403
Executive Director: Terri Brown
Microloan Contact: Charlotte Zietlow, Beth Kuebler
E-mail: tbrown@thestarcenter.com
Tel: 812-339-8937. Fax: 812-335-7352
Service Area: Morgan, Owen, Greene, Lawrence, Monroe,
Brown, and Jackson Bartholomew, Decatur, Jennings
counties.

17 KANSAS

MICROLOAN DEMONSTRATION PROGRAM—KANSAS

Intermediary Lenders

1 South Central Kansas Economic Dev. District, Inc.

209 E. William, Wichita, KS 67202-4012
Executive Director: William Bolin
Microloan Contact: Sam Demel
E-mail: bill@sckedd.org
Tel: (316) 262-7035. Fax: (316) 262-7062
Service Areas: Butler, Chautauqua, Cowley, Elk,
Greenwood, Harper, Harvey, Kingman, Marion,
McPherson, Reno, Rice, Sedgwick and Sumner counties.

2 Center for Business Innovations, Inc.

4747 Troost Avenue, Kansas City, MO 64110
Executive Director: Dale Eltiste Ext. 1201
Micro Contact: Alan Corbet Ext. 1238
E-mail: acorbet@kc-cbi.org
Tel: (816) 561-8567. Fax: (816) 756-1530

Write Action Plan Notes

Service Areas: Wyandotte, Johnson, Douglas, and Leavenworth.

18 KENTUCKY

MICROLOAN DEMONSTRATION PROGRAM—KENTUCKY

Intermediary Lenders

1 Community Ventures Corporation

1450 North Broadway, Lexington, KY 40505
Executive Director: Kevin R. Smith
Microloan Contact: Tyrone Tyra/David Collins
E-mail: cvccorp@prodigy.net
Tel: (606) 231-0054. Fax: (606) 231-0261
Service Area: Anderson, Bourbon, Boyle, Clark, Estill, Fayette, Franklin, Garrard, Harrison, Jessamine, Lincoln, Madison,
Mercer, Nicholas, Powell, Scott, and Woodford counties.

2 Kentucky Highlands Investment Corporation

362 Old Whitley Rd., P.O. Box 1738, London, KY 40743-1738
Executive Director: Jerry Rickett
Microloan Contact: Edgar Davis/Roberta Watkins
E-mail: staylor@khic.org/sthomas@khic.org
Tel: (606) 864-5175. Fax: (606) 864-5194
Service Area: Bell, Clay, Clinton, Cumberland, Estill, Garrard, Harlan, Jackson, Knox, Laurel, Lee, Leslie, Letcher, Lincoln, Madison MCreary, Owsley, Perry, Pulaski, Rockcastle, Russell, Wayne, and Whitley counties.

3 Louisville Central Development Corporation/Business Plus

1407 West Jefferson Street, Suite 200
Louisville, KY 40203

Write Action Plan Notes

Executive Director: Sam Watkins Jr.
Microloan Contact: Kirk Bright—kbright@lcccnews.org
Microloan Contact: Michele Barnett mbarnett@lccc-news.org
E-mail: swatkins@lcccnews.org
Tel:(502)589-1173 Ext. 16
Service Area: Jefferson County/Primary focus Enterprise
Impowerment Zone.

4   Purchase Area Development District

1002 Medical Drive
P.O. Box 588, Mayfield, KY 42066
Executive Director: Henry Hodges
Microloan Contact: Norma Reed-Drouin
E-mail: henry.hodges@mail.state.ky.us
Tel: (270) 247-7171. Fax: (270) 251-6110
Service Area: Ballard, Calloway, Carlisle, Fulton, Graves, Hickman, McCracken and Marshall counties.

20   MASSACHUSETTS

Massachusetts Micro Lenders

1   Economic Dev. Industrial Corp. of Lynn

37 Central Square
3rd Floor
Lynn, MA 01901
Executive Director: Peter M. DeVeau
Microloan Contact: Hal McGaughey
E-mail: pdeveau@broadviewnet.net
Tel: (781) 581-9399
Fax: (781) 581-9731
Service Area: City of Lynn.

Write Action Plan Notes

2   Jewish Vocational Service, Inc.

105 Chauncy Street
6th Floor,
Boston, MA 02111
Executive Director: Barbara Rosenbaum
Microloan Contact: Eric Korsh
E-mail:ekorsh@jvs-boston.org
Tel: (617) 451-8147
Fax: (617) 451-9973
Service Area: Greater Boston with special emphasis on businesses in the Boston Enterprise Zone/Boston Empowerment Zone, and businesses in Mattapan, Dorchester,Roxbury, Hyde Park, and Jamaica Plain.

3   Fall River Office of Economic Development

One Government Center
Fall River, MA 02722
Executive Director: Kenneth Fiola
Microloan Contact: Stephen Parr
E-mail: froedma@aol.com
Tel: (508) 324-2620
Fax: (508) 677-2840
Service Area: City of Fall River.

4   Greater Springfield Entrepreneurial Fund

1176 Main Street
Springfield, MA 01103
Executive Director: James Asselin Ext.227
Microloan Contact: Jim Krzytofik Ext.237
E-mail:jimmya@javanet.com
Tel: (413) 781-6900
Fax (413) 736-0650
Service Area: Hampden County excluding the towns of Chester and Chicopes.

Write Action Plan Notes

5   Community Transportation Association of America

     1341 G Street, NW, Suite 600
     Washington, DC 20005
     Executive Director: Dale J. Marsico
     Microloan Contact: Patrick Kellogg
     E-mail:kellogg@ctaa.org
     Tel: (202) 661-0210
     Fax: (202) 737-9197
     Service Area: North Central Massachusetts—county sub-
     divisions of Athol, Winchendon, Gardner, Templeton,
     Phillipston, Orange, Erving, Wendell, Montague, Gill,
     and Greenfield counties.

6   South Eastern Economic Development Corporation/SEED

     80 Dean Street
     Taunton, MA 02780
     Executive Director: Maria Gooch Smith
     Microloan Contact: Janice Johnson Plumer
     E-mail:SEEDCORP@aol.com
     Tel: (508) 822-1020
     Fax: (508) 880-7869
     Service Areas: SE Massachusetts—Norfolk, Bristol,
     Plymouth, Barnstable, Dukes, and Nantucket counties.

7   Western Massachusetts Enterprise Fund

     P.O. Box 1077
     308 Main Street, Suite 2B
     Greenfield, MA 01302
     Executive Director: Christopher Sikes
     Microloan Contact: Moon Morgan
     E-mail:info@wmef.org
     URL: www.wmef.org
     Tel: (413) 774-4033
     Fax: (413) 774-3673
     Service Area: Berkshire, Franklin, Hampshire, Hampden
     Counties
     and parts of Worcester County.

Write Action Plan Notes

21 MARYLAND

MICROLOAN DEMONSTRATION PROGRAM—MARYLAND

Intermediary Lenders

1   The Development Credit Fund

2526 N. Charles Street, Suite 200, Baltimore, MD 21218
Executive Director: Acknell M. Muldrow, II
Microloan Contact: Erik Johnson
E-mail: erikjson@yahoo.com
Tel: (410) 235-8100. Fax: (410) 235-5899
Service Area: Statewide Maryland excluding Montgomery
and Prince Georges counties.

2   H Street Development Corporation

501 H Street, NE, Washington, DC 20002
Executive Director: William Barrow
Microloan Contact: Yulonda Queen
E-mail: oomhscdc@aol.com
Tel: (202) 544-8353. Fax: (202) 544-3051
Service Area: Montgomery and Prince George's coun-
ties.

22 MAINE

SBA MICROLOAN PROGRAM—MAINE

Intermediary Lenders

1   Coastal Enterprises, Inc

P.O. Box 268 or 36 Water Street, Wiscasset, ME 04578
Executive Director: Ronald Phillips
Microloan Contact: Ellen Golden
E-mail: efg@ceimaine.org or jgs@ceimaine.org
Tel: (207) 882-7552. Fax: (207) 882-7308

Write Action Plan Notes

Service Area: Statewide excluding Aroostock, Piscataquis, Washington, Oxford, Penobscot and Hancock countie.

2   Northern Maine Development Commission

302 South Main St./P.O.B. 779; 1 Caribou, ME 04736
Executive Director: Robert Clark
Microloan Contact: Duane Walton
E-mail: rclark@nmdc.org
Tel: (207) 498-8736. Fax: (207) 493-3108
Service Area: Aroostook.

3   Eastern Maine Development Corporation

One Cumberland Pl., Ste 300, Bangor, ME 04401
Executive Director: David Cole
Microloan Contact: Debbie Metzler
E-mail: dmetzler@emdc.org
Tel: (207) 942-6389. Fax: (207) 942-3548
Service Area: Hancock, Penobscot, Piscataquis, & Washington Counties.

4   Community Concepts, Inc.

P.O.B. 278/19 Market Place, South Paris, ME 04281
Executive Director: Charleen Chase
Microloan Contact: Walter Riseman
E-mail: wriseman@community-concepts.org
Tel: (207) 743-7716. Fax: (207) 743-6513
Service Area: Oxford County.

23 MICHIGAN

MICROLOAN DEMONSTRATION PROGRAM—MICHIGAN

Write Action Plan Notes

Intermediary Lenders

1   Center for Empowerment Economic Development

   2002 Hogback Road, Suite 12
   Ann Arbor, MI 48105
   Executive Director: Michelle Richards
   Microloan Contact: Kellie Long
   E-mail: mrichards@wwnet.net
   Tel: (734) 677-1400. Fax: (734) 677-1465
   Service Area: Macomb, Oakland, Washtenaw and Wayne
   counties (excluding the City of Detroit).

2   Community Capital and Development Corp

   The Walter Reuther Center
   316 West Water Street
   Flint, MI 48503
   Executive Director: Bobby Wells
   Microloan Contact: Bobby Wells
   E-mail: ccdc@tir.com
   Tel: (810) 239-5847. Fax: (810) 239-5575
   Service Area: Genesee County.

3   Kent Area Microbusiness Loan Services

   233 E. Fulton, Suite 101
   Grand Rapids, MI 49503
   Executive Director: Ed Garner
   Microloan Contact: Ed Garner
   E-mail: garnere@kamls.org
   Tel: (616) 771-6880. Fax: (616) 771-8021
   Service Area: Kent County.

4   Northern Initiatives Corp.

   228 West Washington Street
   Marquette, MI 49855
   Executive Director: Dennis West
   Microloan Contact: Todd Horton

Write Action Plan Notes

E-mail:
ni@northerninits.com/todd_horton@northerninits.com
Tel: (906) 228-5571. Fax: (906) 228-5572
Service Area: Upper Peninsula including Alger,
Baraga, Chippewa,Delta, Dickinson, Gogebic, Houghton,
Iron, Keewenaw, Luce, Macinac, Marquette, Menonimee,
Ontonagon, and Schoolcraft counties.

5   Saginaw Economic Development Corporation

301 E. Genesee, 3rd Floor
Saginaw, MI 48607
Commercial Loan Officer: Leslie Weaver
Microloan Contact: Leslie Weaver
E-mail:
Tel: (989) 759-1395. Fax: (989) 754-1715
Service Area: City of Saginaw.

6   Rural Michigan Intermediary Relending Program, Inc.

121 East Front St., Suite 201
Traverse City, MI 49686
Executive Director: Michael Haddad
Microloan Contact: Stephen Spencer
E-mail: mhaddad@timbc.com
Tel: (231) 941-5858. Fax: (231) 941-4616
Service Area: Emmet, Charlevoix, Antrim, Leelanau,
Benzie, Grand Traverse, Kalkaska, Manistee, Wexford,
Missaukee, Cheboygan,Presque Isle, Otsego,
Montmorency, Alpena, Crawford, Oscoda,Alcona,
Roscommon, Ogemaw, Iosco, Osceola, Mason, Lake coun-
ties.

24   MINNESOTA

MICROLOAN DEMONSTRATION PROGRAM—MINNESOTA

Write Action Plan Notes

Intermediary Lenders

1   Northeast Entrepreneur Fund, Inc.

   820 Ninth Street North, Suite 200, Virginia, MN 55792
   Executive Director: Mary Mathews
   Microloan Contact: Bob Voss
   E-mail: info@entrepreneurfund.org
   Tel: (218) 749-4191. Fax: (218) 741-4249
   Service Area: Aitkin, Carlton, Cass, Cook, Crow Wing,
   Itasca, Koochiching, Lake, Pine, and St. Louis coun-
   ties.

2   Women Venture

   2324 University Ave., Suite 200, St. Paul, MN 55112
   Executive Director: Tene Heidelberg
   Microloan Contact: Kim Doverspike
   E-mail: womenven@minn.net
   Tel: (651) 646-3808. Fax: (651)641-7223
   Service Area: Cities of Minneapolis and St. Paul and,
   Andra,
   Carver, Chisago, Dakota, Hennepin, Isanti, Ramsey,
   Scott,
   Washington, and Wright counties.

3   Minneapolis Consortium of Community Developers

   1808 Riverside Ave. S., Suite 206
   Minneapolis, MN 55454-1035
   Executive Director: Ed Lambert
   Microloan Contact: Chistina Jennings
   E-mail: cando@cando.ort
   Tel: (612) 371-9986. Fax: (612) 673-0379
   Service Area: Portions of the City of Minneapolis.

4   Northwest Minnesota Foundation

   4225 Technology Drive, NW, Bemidji, MN 56601
   Executive Director: Jean Downing

Write Action Plan Notes

Microloan Contact: Tim Wang
E-mail: nwmf@paulbunyan.net
Tel: (218) 759-2057. Fax: (218) 759-2328
Service Area: Beltrami, Clearwater, Hubbard, Kittsson, Lake of the Woods, Mahnomen, Marshall, Norman, Pennington, Polk, Red Lake, and Rousseau counties.

25 MISSOURI

MICROLOAN DEMONSTRATION PROGRAM—MISSOURI

Intermediary Lenders

1   Center for Business Innovation, Inc.

4747 Troost Avenue, Kansas City, MO 64110
Executive Director: Dale Eltiste
Microloan Contact: Alan Corbet
E-mail: deltiste@kc-cbi.org
Tel: (816) 561-8567. Fax: (816) 756-1530
Service Area: Platte, Jackson, Clay and Cass counties.

2   Justine Petersen Housing and Reinvestment Corporation

5031 Northrup Avenue
St. Louis, MO 63110
Executive Director: Robert Boyle
Microloan Contact: Sheri Flanigan-Vazquez
E-mail: sflanigan@justinepetersen.org
Tel: (314) 664-5051, ext. 117 Fax (314) 664-5364
Service Area: Counties of Franklin, Jefferson, Lincoln, St. Charles, St. Louis,Warren, and the City of St. Louis.

3   Rural Missouri, Incorporated

1014 Northeast Drive
Jefferson City, MO 65109

Write Action Plan Notes

Executive Director: Ken Lueckenotte
Microloan Contact: Karie Mengwasser (573)635-0136
E-mail: karie@rmiinc.org
Tel: (573) 635-0136 Fax (573) 635-5636
Service Area: Statewide excluding Platte, Jackson, Clay and
Cass counties.

26 MISSISSIPPI

Microloan Program In Mississippi

The MicroLoan Program provides small loans ranging from $100 to $35,000. Under this program, the SBA makes funds available to nonprofit intermediaries; these, in turn, make the loans. The average loan size is $10,000. Interest rates vary, depending upon the intermediary lender. Rates are generally competitive. This program is available at limited number locations.

USE OF PROCEEDS—Microloans may be used to finance furniture, machinery, equipment, fixtures, inventory, and/or working capital.

There are two intermediary lenders in the State of Mississippi:

1   Friends of Children of Mississippi, Inc.

    4880 McWillie Circle
    Jackson, Mississippi 39206
    Contact: Marvin Hogan or Sandra Edwards
    Tel: (601) 362-1541
    Fax: (601) 362-1613
    Service Area: All counties.

2   Southern Financial Partners

    605 Main Street, Suite 203
    Arkadelphia, AR 71923

Write Action Plan Notes

Contact: Ms. Bryn Bagwell, Senior Lender
Tel: (870) 246-9739
Service Area: Northwest counties in Mississippi.

There are SBA loans to fit just about everyone's needs.
For more details—call (601) 965-4378.

27   MONTANA

MICROLOAN DEMONSTRATION PROGRAM MONTANA

1   Montana Community Development Corp

103 East Main, Missoula, MT 59802
Contact: Charlie Wright
Tel: (406) 728-9234
Service Area: Lake, Mineral, Missoula, Ravalli, and Sanders counties.

28   NORTH CAROLINA

MICROLOAN PROGRAM—NORTH CAROLINA

Microloans were developed to increase the availability of very small loans to prospective small business borrowers. Under this program, the SBA makes funds available to non-profit intermediaries which, in turn, make loans to eligible borrowers in amounts that range from $100 to a maximum of $35,000.
The average loan size is $10,500.
In addition to microloans, the intermediaries are also required to provide business based technical assistance and training to their microborrowers.

The maximum term for a microloan is 6 years. However, loan terms vary according to the size of the loan, the planned use of funds, the requirements of the intermediary lender, and the needs of the small business borrower. Interest rates vary, depending on the lender and its costs to the

Write Action Plan Notes

U.S. Treasury. Collateral—Each intermediary lender has its own requirements for extending credit and generally requires some type of collateral, and a personal guaranty from the business owner. In addition to microloans, intermediaries are required to provide technical assistance and training to their microborrowers.

North Carolina Intermediary Lenders

1   Self-Help Ventures Fund

    301 W Main St
    PO Box 3619
    Durham, NC 27701
    Tel: (919) 956-4400. Fax: (919) 956-4600
    email: bob@self-help.org
    Service Area: Statewide excluding Watauga, Avery, Mitchell, and Yancey counties.

2   Self-Help Eastern Regional Office

    101 W 14th St, Ste 200
    Greenville NC 27834
    Tel:(800) 893-9669
    Fax: (252) 752-0121

3   Self-Help Triad Regional Office

    122 N Elm St, Ste 810
    Greensboro NC 27401
    Tel:(800) 269-7426
    Fax: (336) 378-0518

4   Self-Help Charlotte Regional Office

    926 Elizabeth Ave, Ste 302
    Charlotte NC 28204
    Tel: (800) 394-7428
    Fax: (704) 375-5703

Write Action Plan Notes

5   Self-Help Western Regional Office

     34 Wall St, Ste. 502
     sheville NC 28801
     Tel:(800) 229-7428
     Fax:(828) 253-7781

6   Self-Help Wilmington Branch

     210 N Front St, Ste 714
     Wilmington NC 28401
     Tel:(910) 341-3272
     Fax: (910) 341-3270

7   W.A.M.Y. Community Action, Inc.

     PO Box 552
     Boone, NC 28607
     Tel: (828) 264-2421
     Fax: (828) 264-0952
     email: wamyloans@boone.net
     Service Area: Watauga, Avery, Mitchell, and Yancey
     counties.

8   Neuse River Development Authority, Inc.

     233 Middle St
     PO Box 1111
     New Bern, NC 28563
     Tel: (252) 638-6724. Fax: 252-638-1819
     email: lriter@nrda.org
     Service Areas: Craven, Carteret, Duplin,
     Jones, Greene, Lenoir, Johnston, Wayne, Onslow,
     Pamlico.
     URL: http://www.nrda.org

29   NORTH DAKOTA

MICROLOAN DEMONSTRATION PROGRAM—NORTH DAKOTA

Write Action Plan Notes

Intermediary Lenders

1   Lake Agassiz Regional Council

    417 Main Avenue, Fargo, ND 58103
    Contact: Sue Hartmann
    Tel: (701)239-5373 Fax: (701)235-6706
    Service Area: Nationwide.

2   Dakota Certified Development Corporation

    51 Broadway, Suite 400
    Fargo, ND 58102
    Tel: (701) 293-8892 or (800)611-8997
    Fax: (701)293-7819

3   700 East Main AVenue

    Bismarck, ND 58502
    Tel: (701)328-5851
    Fax: (701)250-4304
    Service Area: Nationwide.

30   NEBRASKA

MICROLOAN DEMONSTRATION PROGRAM—NEBRASKA

Intermediary Lenders

1   Rural Enterprise Assistance Project-Center for Rural
    Affairs

    101 South Tallman Street
    P.O.Box 406, Walthill, NE 68067
    Executive Director: Don Ralston
    Microloan Contact: Kendall Scheer
    E-mail: kendalls@cfra.org
    Tel: (402) 846-5428. Fax: (402) 846-5420
    Service Area: Antelope, Banner, Blaine, Boone, Box
    Butte, Boyd, Brown, Burt, Cass, Cedar, Cherry,

Write Action Plan Notes

Cheyenne, Colfax, Custer, Dawes, Deuel, Dixon, Gage, Garden, Garfield, Greeley, Holt, Jefferson, Johnson, Keya Paha, Kimball, Knox, Lancaster, Loup, McPherson, Morrill, Nance, Nemaha, Otoe, Pawnee, Pierce, Platte, Richardson, Rock, Saline, Saunders, Seward, Sheridan, Sioux, Scottsbluff, Thurston, Wayne, and Wheeler counties.

2   West Central Nebraska Development District, Inc.

201 East 2nd Street, Suite C
P.O. Box 599, Ogailala, NE 69153
Executive Director: Martin O'Haus
Microloan Contact: Vyla Brown
E-mail: mowcndd@lakemac.net/vbwcndd@lakemac.net
Tel: (308) 284-6077. Fax: (308) 284-6070
Service Area: Arthur, Chase, Dawson, Dundy, Frontier, Furnas, Gosper, Grant, Hayes, Hitchcock, Hooker, Keith, Lincoln, Logan, Perkins, Red Willow, Thomas, and McPherson counties.

TECHNICAL ASSISTANCE GRANT RECIPIENTS

3   New Mexico Community Development Loan Fund

P.O. Box 705, 700 4th St., SW, Albuquerque, NM 87102-0705
Executive Director: Vangie Gabaldon
Microloan Contact: Rockling Todea
E-mail: vgnmcdlf@aol.com
Tel: (505) 243-3196. Fax: (505) 243-8803
Service Area: Nationwide.

31 NEW HAMPSHIRE

MICROLOAN DEMONSTRATION PROGRAM—NEW HAMPSHIRE

Write Action Plan Notes

Intermediary Lenders

1   Northern Community Investment Corp.

    20 Main Street or P.O. Box 904,
    St. Johnsbury, VT 05819
    Executive Director: Carol Walker
    Microloan Contact: Michael Tragakiss
    E-mail: carol@ncic.org
    Tel: (802) 748-5101. Fax: (802) 748-1884
    Service Area: Grafton, Carol and Coos counties.

MICROLOAN DEMONSTRATION PROGRAM—NEW JERSEY

Intermediary Lenders

2   Cooperative Business Assistance Corporation

    328 Market Street
    Camden, NJ 08102
    Executive Director: R. Michael Diemer
    Microloan Contact: R. Michael Diemer
    E-mail: hstonecbac2000@aol.com
    Tel: (856) 966-8181. Fax: (856) 966-0036
    Service Area: Camden, Gloucester, Atlantic, Cape May,
    Cumberland, and Salem Counties.

3   Greater Newark Business Development Consortium

    271 B South Orange Avenue
    Newark, NJ 07103
    Executive Director: David Means
    Microloan Contact: Frank McIver
    Tel: (973) 242-4404. Fax: (973) 242-0485
    Service Area: Bergen, Essex, Hudson, Middlesex,
    Monmouth,
    Morris, Passaic, Sussex, and Ocean counties.

Write Action Plan Notes

4   Community Lending & Investment Corp. of Jersey

30 Montgomery St.
Jersey City, NY 07302
Executive Director: Thomas Ahern
Microloan Contact: John Rogers
Tel: (201) 333-7797. Fax: (201) 946-9367
Service Area: City of Jersey City.

5   Trenton Business Assistance Corp.

247 E. Front Street
Trenton, NJ 08611
Executive Director: Deborah Osgood
Microloan Contact: Russ Haas
E-mail: tbacsba@earthlink.net/mfguberman@ad.com
Tel: (609) 396-2595. Fax: (609) 396-2598
Service Area: portions of the City of Trenton,
Mercer, Middlesex, and Burlington, Hunterdon, Warren,
and Phillipsburg Counties.

6   Union County Economic Development Corp

Liberty Hall Corporate Center
1085 Morris Avenue, Suite 531,
Union, NJ 07083
Executive Director: Maureen Tinen
Microloan Contact: Carlos N. Sanchez
E-mail: afarrah@ucedc.com
Tel: (908) 527-1166. Fax: (908) 527-1207
Service Area: Union and Somerset Counties.

32   NEW MEXICO

MICROLOAN DEMONSTRATION PROGRAM—NEW MEXICO

Write Action Plan Notes

Intermediary Lenders

1   Women's Economic Self Sufficiency Team

    414 Silver SW, Albuquerque, NM 87102-3239
    Contact: Agnes Noonan
    Tel: (505) 241-4753. Fax: (505) 241-4766
    Service Area: Nationwide.

33   NEVADA

MICROLOAN DEMONSTRATION PROGRAM—NEVADA

Intermediary Lenders

1   Nevada Microenterprise Initiative

    116 East 7th Street, Suite 1
    Carson City, NV 89701-5236
    Tel: (775) 841-1420. Fax: (775) 841-2221

2   Nevada Microenterprise Initiative

    113 West Plumb Lane
    Reno, NV 89509
    Tel: (775) 324-1812. Fax: (775) 324-1813

3   Nevada Microenterprise Initiative

    1600 East Desert Inn Road, Suite 203
    Las Vegas, NV 89101
    Tel: (702) 734-3555. Fax: (702) 734-3530
    Executive Director: Nancy Erends Bahr
    Microloan Contact: Anna Siefert
    E-mail: asiefert@4microbiz.org
    Website: http://www.4microbiz.org

Write Action Plan Notes

34 NEW YORK

MICROLOAN DEMONSTRATION PROGRAM—NEW YORK

Intermediary Lenders

1   Adirondack Economic Development Corporation

   Trudeau Road, P.O.B. 747, Saranac Lake, NY 12983
   Executive Director: Ernest Hohmeyer
   Microloan Contact: Ernest Hohmeyer
   E-mail: aedc-patrick@northnet.org
   Tel: (518) 891-5523. Fax: (518) 891-9820
   Service Area: Clinton, Essex, Franklin, Fulton,
   Hamilton, Herkimer, Jefferson, Lewis, Oneida, Oswego,
   St. Lawrence, Saratoga, Warren and Washington counties.

2   Columbia Hudson Partnership.

   444 Warren Street, Hudson, NY 12534-2415
   Executive Director: David Pearce
   Microloan Contact: David Pearce
   E-mail: 76072.2771@compuserve.com
   Tel: (518) 828-4718. Fax: (518) 828-0901
   Service Area: Columbia County.

3   Manhattan Borough Development Corp.

   55 John Street, 17th Floor New York, NY 10038
   Executive Director: Ollie Chatman
   Microloan Contact: Marta Gomez
   E-mail: ochapman@mbdc.org
   Tel: (212) 791-3660. Fax: (212) 571-0873
   Service Area: The borough of Manhattan.

4   Rural Opportunities Enterprise Center, Inc.

   400 East Avenue, Rochester, NY 14607
   Executive Director: Lee Beaulac
   Microloan Contact: Joan Dallis

Write Action Plan Notes

E-mail: jdallis@ruralinc.org
Tel: (716) 340-3344. Fax: (716) 340-3326
Service Area: Onandaga, Ulster, Monroe, Schuyler, Chemung,
Allegheny, Cattaraugua, Cayuga, Chatauqua, Dutchess, Erie,
Genessee, Greene, Livingston, Niagara, Ontario, Orange, Orleans,
Putnam, Seneca, Steuben, Sullivan, Wayne, Wyoming, and Yates counties.

5   Community Development Corporation of Long Island

2100 Middle Country Rd. Suite 300
Centereach, NY 11720
Executive Director: Wilbur Klatsky
Microloan Contact: Trevor Davis
e-mail: trevorcdc@aol.com
Tel: (631) 471-1215. Fax: (631)471-1210
Service Area: Suffolk and Nassau Counties.

6   New York Association for New Americans, Inc.

17 Battery Place
New York, NY 10004
Executive Director: Mark Handelman
Microloan Contact: Yanki Tshering
E-mail: mhandelm@nyana.org
Tel: (212) 425-5051. Fax: (212)425-7260
Service Area: The borough of Queens.

7   Alternatives Fed. Credit Union

301 W. State Street
Ithaca, NY 14850
Executive Director: William Myers
Microloan Contact: Deirdre Silverman
E-mail:
Tel: (607) 273-3582. Fax: (607) 277-6391

Write Action Plan Notes

Service Area: Schuyler, Tompkins, Tioga, Cortland, Chemung,
and Broome counties.

8   Buffalo Economic Renaissance Corporation

617 Main Street
Buffalo, NY 14203
Tel: (716) 847-LOAN (5626)
E-mail website: www.growbfo.org
Service Area: City of Buffalo.

9   Erie County Industrial Development Agency

275 Oak Street
Buffalo, New York 14202
Tel: (716) 847-LOAN (5626)
E-mail website: www.edidany.com
Service Area: Erie County Only.

35   OHIO

MICROLOAN DEMONSTRATION PROGRAM—OHIO

Intermediary Lenders

1   Community Capital Development Corp.

900 Michigan Avenue, Columbus, OH 43215-1165
Executive Director: Brad Shimp
Microloan Contact: Stephen Hikida
E-mail: stephen.hikida@ccdcorp.org,
brad.shimp@ccdcorp.org
Tel: (614) 645-3799, (888) 756-2232. Fax: (614) 645-8588
Service Area: City of Columbus, Franklin, Delaware, Fairfield,
Licking, Fayette, Madison, Pickaway and Union Counties.

Write Action Plan Notes

2   Enterprise Development Corporation

9030 Hocking Hills Drive
The Plains, OH 45780-1209
Executive Director: Daniel Dusterburg
Microloan Contact: Lisa Canode
E-mail: edc@seorf.ohiou.edu
Tel: (740) 797-9646. Fax: (740) 797-9659
Service Area: Adams, Ashland, Athens, Belmont, Brown, Carroll,
Columbiana, Coshocton, Gallia, Guernsey, Harrison, Highland, Holmes, Jackson, Jefferson, Knox, Lawrence, Meigs, Monroe, Morgan, Muskingum, Hocking, Noble, Perry, Pike, Ross, Scioto, Tuscarawas, Vinton, Washington, and Hocking counties.

3   Hamilton County Development Co.

1776 Mentor Avenue, Cincinnati, OH 45212
Executive Director: David Main
Microloan Contact: Lou Ann Walden
E-mail: lawalden@hcdc.com
Tel: (513) 631-8292. Fax: (513) 631-4887
Service Area: City of Cincinnati, Adams, Brown, Butler, Clermont, Clinton, Hamilton, Warren, and Highland counties.

4   Women's Org. for Mentoring, Entrepreneurship, & Networking

526 S. Main Street, Suite 235
Akron, OH 44311-1058
Executive Director: Janice Robinson
Microloan Contact: Janice Robinson
E-mail: women@ald.net
Tel: (330) 379-9280. Fax: (330) 379-3454
Service Area: Cuyahoga, Lake, Lorain, Mahoning, Medina, Stark, Summit, and Wayne counties.

Write Action Plan Notes

5   Kent Regional Business Alliance

     College of Business #300-A, KSU
     Kent, OH 44242
     Executive Director: Linda Yost
     Microloan Contact: Toni Brion
     E-mail: lyost@bsa3.kent.edu
     Tel: (330)672-2772. Fax: (330)672-9338
     Service Areas: Ashtabula, Geauga, Trumbull, Portage,
     Columbiana, Carroll, Holmes, Coshocton, Tuscarawas,
     and Harrison counties.

36   OKLAHOMA

MICROLOAN DEMONSTRATION PROGRAM—OKLAHOMA

Participating Intermediary Lenders

1   Greenwood Community Development Corp.

     131 N. Greenwood Ave., 2nd Floor
     Tulsa, OK 74120
     Tel: 918/585-2084
     Contact: Reuben Gant, Executive Director
     Area of Operation: Northwest Tulsa County

2   Rural Enterprises of Oklahoma, Inc.

     P.O. Box 1335
     Durant, OK 74702
     Tel: 580/924-5094
     Contact: Debbie Partin, Director/Fin. Serv.
     Area of Operation: Nationwide.

3   Tulsa Economic Development Corp.

     907 S. Detroit Ave., Suite 1001
     Tulsa, OK 74120
     Tel: 918/585-8332
     Contact: Rose M. Washington-Rentie, Exec. Dir.

Write Action Plan Notes

Area of Operation: Adair, Canadian, Cherokee, Cleveland, Craig, Creek, Delaware, Haskell, Hughes, Kay, Latimer, LeFlore, Lincoln, Logan, Mayes, McIntosh, Muskogee, Noble, Nowata, Okfuskee, Oklahoma, Okmulgee, Osage, Ottawa, Pawnee, Payne, Pittsburg, Pottawatomie, Rogers, Seminole, Sequoyah, Wagoner,
Washington Counties, and City of Tulsa.

37 PORTLAND

PORTLAND DISTRICT OFFICE

MICRO-LOAN PROGRAM INTERMEDIARY LENDERS

1   Cascades West Financial Services, Inc.

1400 Queen Ave SE, Suite 205C
PO Box 686
Albany, OR 97321
Contact: Diane Searle—Microloan Coordinator
Tel: (541) 924-8480
Toll Free: (877) 794-6607 or (800) 638-0750
Fax: (541) 967-4651
Email: dsearle@ocwcog.org
Website: http://www.cascadeswest.com/microloan.htm
Counties Served: Benton, Clackamas, Hood River, Jefferson,
Lane, Lincoln, Linn, Marion, Multnomah, Polk, Tillamook, Wasco, Washington, Yamhill.

2   Oregon Association of Minority Entrepreneurs Credit Corporation

4134 N Vancouver Avenue
Portland, OR 97217
Contact: Sanford Maddox & Lisa Stein
Tel: (503) 249-7744
Fax: (503) 249-2027
Email: oame@uswest.net
Website: http://www.oame.org
Counties Served:

Write Action Plan Notes

In   Oregon: Clackamas,   Clatsop,   Columbia,   Hood,
Multnomah, Tillamook, Washington
In Washington: Clark

3   SOWAC Business Training & Lending Center

33 N Central Ave, Suite 209
Medford, OR 97501
Contact: Dennis Davis—Loan Fund Manager
Tel: (541) 779-3992
Fax: (541) 779-5195
Email: dpdavis@sowac.org
Website: http://www.sowac.org
Counties Served: Jackson, Josephine, Klamath, Lake.

4   Umpqua Community Development Corporation

738 SE Kane Street
Roseburg, OR 97470
Contact: Bob Ault
Tel: (541) 673-4909
Fax: (541) 673-5023
Email: rault@mcsi.net
Counties Served: Coos, Curry, Douglas.

38   PENNSYLVANIA

MICROLOAN DEMONSTRATION PROGRAM—PENNSYLVANIA

Intermediary Lenders

1   The Ben Franklin Tech. Center of SE Pennsylvania

11 Penn Center 1835 Market St Ste 1100,
Phil, PA 19103
President & CEO: Rose Ann Rosenthal
Microloan Contact: Leslie Esdaile/Scott Booker
E-mail: bftc@benfranklin.org
Tel: (215) 972-6700. Fax No. (215) 972-5588
Service Area: Bucks, Chester, Delaware, Montgomery,
and Philadelphia counties.

Write Action Plan Notes

2   Community Loan Fund of Southwestern PA, Inc.

425 Sixth Avenue, Ste. 260,
Pittsburgh, PA 15219
Executive Director: Mark Peterson
Microloan Contact: Mark Peterson/Marcia Lynch
E-mail: mbevan@clfund.com
Tel: (412) 201-2450. Fax No. (412) 201-2451
Service Area: Allegheny, Armstong, Beaver, Butler and Indiana counties.

3   The Washington County Council on Economic Development

100 West Beau St., Ste. 703,
Washington, PA 15301-4432
Executive Director: Malcolm Morgan
Microloan Contact: Ray Grudi/Bev Wilson
E-mail: wcced@pulsenet.com
Tel: (724) 228-6949. Fax: (724) 250-6502
Service Area: Southwestern area of Pennsylvania including Greene, Fayette, Washington, Westmoreland, Preston Counties.

4   Philadelphia Commercial Development Corporation

1315 Walnut Street, Suite 600
Philadelphia, PA 19107
Executive Director: Curtis Jones, Jr.
Microloan Contact: Rick Dean
E-mail: econpcdc@aol.com
Tel: (215) 790-2210. Fax: (215) 790-2222
Service Area: Philadelphia, Bucks, Chester, Delaware, and
Montgomery counties.

5   MetroAction, Inc.

222 Mulberry Street, P.O. Box 4731
Scranton, PA 18501-0431
President: John Kokinchak

Write Action Plan Notes

Microloan Contact: Kristine French
E-mail: kfrench@scrantonchamber.com
Tel: (570) 342-7711. Fax: (570) 347-6262
Service Area: Luzerne, Lackawanna, and Monroe counties.

6   Northwest Pennsylvania Regional Planning & Dev.
Commission

395 Seneca Street
Oil City, PA 16301
Executive Director: William Steiner
Microloan Contact: Dale F. Massie
E-mail: dalem@nwplan.org
Tel: (814) 677-4800. Fax: (814) 677-7663
Service Area: Clarion, Crawford, Erie, Forest,
Lawrence,
Mercer, Warren and Verangro counties.

7   Southern Alleghenies Planning & Development
Commission

541-58th Street
Altoona, Pennsylvania 16602
Executive Director: Edward M. Silvetti
Microloan Contact: Michael Mignogna
E-mail: sapdc@sapdc.org
Tel: (814) 949-6520. Fax: (814) 949-6505
Service Area: Bedford, Blair, Cambria, Fulton, Huntingdon,
and Somerset counties.

39 PUERTO RICO

SBA MICROLOAN PROGRAM—Puerto Rico

Intermediary Lenders

1   Corporación para el Fomento de la Ciudad Capital
(COFECC)

Write Action Plan Notes

Ave. Muñoz Rivera, #1103, Río Piedras, PR 00926
Contact: Carlos Gabriel Santiago
Telephone: (787) 756-5080. Fax: (787) 753-8960
Service Area: Nationwide.

40   RHODE ISLAND

SBA MICROLOAN PROGRAM—Rhode Island

Intermediary Lenders

1   Rhode Island Coalition for Minority Investment

216 Weybosset Street, 2nd Floor
Providence, RI 02903
Executive Director: Denise Barge
Microloan Contact: Henry Reid
E-mail: dbarge.midc@efortress.com
Telephone: (401) 351-2999. Fax: (401) 351-0990
Service Areas: Nationwide

41   SOUTH CAROLINA

South Carolina District Office

Microloan Demonstration Program

Intermediary Lenders:

1   Business Carolina, Inc.

1441 Main Street, Suite 900
Columbia, SC 29201
Tel: (803) 461-3801
Fax: (803) 461-3826
www.businesscarolina.net

Write Action Plan Notes

Charleston Citywide Local Development Corporation

75 Calhoun St., 3rd Floor
Charleston, SC 29403
Tel: (803) 724-3796
Fax: (803) 724-7354
Service Area: City of Charleston.

42   SOUTH DAKOTA

MICROLOAN DEMONSTRATION PROGRAM—SOUTH DAKOTA

Intermediary Lenders

1   Lakota Fund

P.O.Box 340 or Trade Center,
Kyle, South Dakota 57752
Executive Director: Elsie Meeks
Microloan Contact: Monica Perkildsen
E-mail: monica@rapidnet.com
Tel: (605) 455-2500. Fax: (605) 455-2585
Service Area: Bennett County, Pine Ridge Indian
Reservation, and areas of Shannon and Jackson coun-
ties which are surrounded by Indian Lands, and exclu-
sive of Northern Jackson County.

2   NE South Dakota Economic Corporation

414 Third Avenue, East, Sisseton, SD 57262-1598
Executive Director: Robert Hull
Microloan Contact: Carla Schweitzer
E-mail: nesdec@dtgnet.com
Tel: (605) 698-7654 Fax: (605) 698-3038
Service Area: Beadle, Brown, Buffalo, Campbell,
Clark, Codington, Day, Edmunds, Faulk, Grant, Hand,
Hyde, Jerauld, Kingsbury, McPherson, Marshall, Miner,
Potter, Roberts, Sanborn, Spink, and Walworth coun-
ties.

Write Action Plan Notes

43   TENNESSEE

MICROLOAN DEMONSTRATION PROGRAM—TENNESSEE

Intermediary Lenders

1   Southeast Community Capital

   1020 Commerce Park Drive
   Oak Ridge, TN 37830
   Executive Director: Tom Rogers
   Microloan Contact: David Bradshaw
   E-mail: info@tech2020.org
   Tel: (865) 220-2025. Fax: (865) 220-2030
   Service Area: All counties in Tennessee.

2   Economic Ventures, Inc.

   1545 Western Ave., Ste. 5
   Knoxville, TN 37921-3550
   Executive Director: Melissa Muendel
   Microloan Contact: Vickie Riggs
   E-mail: vriggs@evitn.org/mmccay@kcdc.gov
   Tel: (865) 524-0360 Ext 102. Fax: (865) 524-3437
   Service Area: Anderson, Blount, Campbell, Clairborne,
   Cocke, Grainger, Hamblen, Jefferson, Knox, Loudon,
   Monroe, Morgan, Roane, Scott, Sevier, Union, Greene,
   Hancock, Hawkins, Sullivan, Washington, Johnson,
   Carter, and Unicoi counties.

3   LeMoyne-Owen College Community Development Corp.

   802 Walker Avenue, Suite Five
   Memphis, TN 38126
   Executive Director: Jeffery Higgs
   Tel: (901) 942-6265
   Service Area: Shelby County—Memphis, TN area.

Write Action Plan Notes

44 TEXAS

MICROLOAN DEMONSTRATION PROGRAM—TEXAS

Intermediary Lenders

1   ACCION Texas

2014 S. Hackberry,
San Antonio, TX 78210
President/CEO: Janie Barrera
Microloan Contact: Elizabeth Montoya
E-Mail: info@acciontexas.org
Tel: (210) 226-3664
Fax: (210) 226-533-2940
Service Area: Aransas, Atascosa, Bandera, Bastrop, Bee, Bexar,Blanco, Brewster, Brooks, Burnet, Caldwell, Calhoun, Cameron, Comal,Concho, Crocket, Culberson, Dallas, DeWitt, Dimmit, Duval, Edwards,El Paso, Fayette, Frio, Gillespie, Goliad, Gonzales, Guadalupe, Harris, Hays, Hidalgo, Hudspeth, Irion, Jackson, Jeff Davis,Jim Wells, Karnes, Kendall, Kenedy, Kerr, Kimble, Kinney, Kleberg, Lampasas, LaSalle, Lavaca, Lee, Live Oak, Llano, Loving, Mason, Maverick, McCulloch, McMullen, Medina, Menard, Midland, Nueces, Pecos, Presidio, Real, Reeves, Refugio, San Patricio, San Saba, Schleicher, Starr, Sutton, Tarrant, Tom Green, Travis, Uvalde, Val Verde, Victoria, Webb, Willacy, Zapata, and Zavala Counties.

2   Business Invest In Growth (BiG)

912 Bastrop Hwy., Suite 210
Austin, TX 78741
President: Jeannette Peten
Microloan Contact: Jeannette Peten
E-mail: big@rocketmail.com
Tel: (512) 928-8010. Fax: (512) 926-2997

Write Action Plan Notes

Service Area: Bastrop, Blanco, Burleson, Burnet,
Gillespie, Hays,Lampasas, Lee, Llano, Mason, Milam,
McCulloch, San Saba, Travis, and Williamson Counties.

3   Business Resource Center Incubator

401 Franklin Avenue,
Waco, TX 76701
Executive Director: John Dosher
Microloan Contact: John Dosher
E-mail: john@brc-waco.com
Tel: (254) 754-8898. Fax: (254) 756-0776
Service Area: Bell, Bosque, Coryell, Falls, Hill,
and McLennan counties.

4   The Corporation for Economic Development of Harris
County

2223 West Loop South, Suite 400,
Houston, TX 77027-5926
Executive Director: Amos Brown
Microloan Contact: Janis Fowler
E-mail: jfowler@hchcda.co.harris.tx.us
Tel: (713) 840-8804. Fax: (713) 840-8806
Service Area: Brazoria, Chambers, Fort Bend,
Galveston,
Harris, Liberty, Montgomery, and Waller Counties.

5   Neighborhood Housing Services of Dimmit County

301 Pena Street
Carrizo Springs, Texas 78834
Executive Director: Manual Estrada, Jr.
Microloan Contact:
E-Mail: nhsdc@brushco.net
Tel: (830) 876-5295. Fax: (830) 876-4136
Service Area: Dimmit, Kinney, LaSalle, Maverick,
Real,
Uvalde, Val Verde and Zavala Counties.

Write Action Plan Notes

6   Rural Development and Finance Corporation

711 Navarro Street, Suite 350
San Antonio, TX 78205
Executive Director: Gloria Guerrero
Microloan Contact: Lucy Brooks
E-Mail: RDFC@DCCI.COM
Tel: (210) 212-4552. Fax: (210) 212-9159
Service Area: Cameron, Dimmit, El Paso, Hidalgo, Maverick,
Webb, Zapata, and Zavala Counties.

7   San Antonio Local Development Corp.

215 S. San Saba, Rm 107
San Antonio, TX 78207
Executive Director: Ramiro A. Cavazos
Microloan Contact: Robert Ayala
E-mail: roberta@sanantonio.gov
Tel: (210) 207-3930. Fax: (210) 207-3939
Service Area: Atascosa, Bandera, Bexar, Comal, Frio, Gillespie,
Guadalupe, Karnes, Kendall, Kerr, Medina, and Wilson Counties.

8   Southern Dallas Development Corporation

1402 Corinth, Suite 1150,
Dallas, TX 75215
Executive Director: Jim Reid
Microloan Contact: Charles English
E-mail: cwheeler@sddc.org
Tel: (214) 428-7332. Fax: (214) 426-6847
Service Area: Portions of the City of Dallas.

45   UTAH

MICROLOAN DEMONSTRATION PROGRAM—UTAH

Write Action Plan Notes

Intermediary Lenders

1   Utah Technology Finance Corporation

177 East 100 South, Salt Lake City, UT 84111
Executive Director: F. Duane Blackley
Microloan Contact: Shane Knighton
E-mail: sknighton@utfc.org
Tel: (801) 741-4200. Fax: (801) 741-4249
Service Area: Nationwide

46   VERMONT

MICROLOAN DEMONSTRATION PROGRAM—VERMONT

Participating Micro Lenders
The Microloan Program provides small loans ranging from
under $500 to $35,000.

1   Economic Dev. Council of Northern Vermont, Inc.

155 Lake Street, St. Albans, VT 05478
Contact: Connie Stanley-Little
Tel: (802) 524-4546. Fax: (802) 527-1081
Service Area: Chittenden, Franklin, Grand Isle,
Lamoille, and Washington counties.

2   Northern Community Investments Corporation

20 Main St., P.O. Box 904, St. Johnsbury, VT 05819
Contact: Paul Denton
Tel: (802) 748-5101. Fax: (802) 748-1884
Service Area: Caledonia, Essex, and Orleans counties.

3   Vermont Development Credit Union

18 Pearl Street, Burlington, VT 05401
Contact: Dede Schlageter
Tel: (802) 865-3404. Fax: (802) 862-8971

Write Action Plan Notes

Service Area: Addison, Bennington, Orange, Rutland, Windham counties.

PRE QUALIFICATION LOAN PROGRAM

The SBA prequalification loan program is available to businesses owned 51% or more by women, veterans, or minorities. If approved the borrower receives an SBA committment letter and seeks a competitive lender to provide the SBA guaranteed loan.

1   Green Mountain Economic Development Corp.

24 Mill St., North Hartland, VT 05052
Contact: Jim Saudale
Tel: (802) 295-3710. Fax (802) 295-3779
Service Area: Nationwide

MICRO BUSINESS DEVELOPMENT PROGRAM

The Micro Business Development Program offers counseling services to income eligible Vermonters who own or intend to start a small business.

Vermont	Champlain Valley Office of Econ. Opportunity 431 Pine Street, Burlington, VT 05401 Contact: Jim White Tel: (802) 860-1417. Fax: (802) 860-1387 Service Area: Addison,Grand Isle, Franklin, Chittenden
Vermont	Central VT Community Action 195 US Route 302, Barre, VT 05641 Contact: Carol Flint Tel: (800) 639-1053. Fax: (802) 479-5353 Service Area: lamoille, Orange, Washington counties.

Write Action Plan Notes

Vermont   Northeast Kingdom Community Action
                                    108 Cherry Street, St. Johnsbury, VT
                                    05819
                                    Contact: Don Welch
                                    Tel: (800) 639-4065. Fax: (802) 748-0732
                                    Service Area: Caledonia, Essex, and
                                    Orleans counties.

Vermont   Southwestern VT Community Action
                                    60 Center Street, Rutland, VT 05701
                                    Contact: Michelle Rock
                                    Tel: (800) 717-2762. Fax: (802) 775-
                                    9949
                                    Service Area: Bennington & Rutland
                                    counties.

Vermont   Southeastern VT Community Action
                                    213 Gage Street, Bellows Falls, VT
                                    05101
                                    Contact: Pat Apicella
                                    Tel: (877) 963-2568. Fax: (802) 722-
                                    4509
                                    Service Area: Windsor & Windham
                                    counties.

47 VIRGINIA

MICROLOAN DEMONSTRATION PROGRAM—VIRGINIA

Intermediary Lenders

Virginia   Business Development Centre, Inc.
                                    147 Mill Ridge Road
                                    Lynchburg, VA 24502
                                    Executive Director: Catherine McFaden
                                    Microloan Contact: Rich Stallings
                                    E-mail: rich@lbdc.com
                                    Tel: (434) 582-6100. Fax: (434)
                                    582-6106

Write Action Plan Notes

Service Area: Counties of Amherst, Appomattox, Bedford, Campell, and the Cities of Bedford and Lynchburg, and the Towns of Altavista and Amherst.
Website: http://www.lbdc.com

Virginia

Center for Community Development
440 High Street, Suite 204
Portsmouth, VA 23704
Executive Director: Bruce Asberry
Microloan Contact: Monique Harrell
E-mail: profit1@pilot.infi.net
Tel: (757) 399-0925 Fax: (757) 399-2642
Service Area: Cities of Chesapeake, Hampton, Newport News, Norfolk, Portsmouth, Suffolk, Virginia Beach.

Center for Community Development
c/o Norfolk Redevelopment and Housing Authority
201 Granby Street, 6th Floor
Norfolk, VA 23510
Contact: Ms. Suzanne Ramus-Jones
Tel: (757) 623-1111 Ext 323. Fax: (757) 626-1607 Email: profit6@pilot.infi.net

Center for Community Development
c/o Hampton University Business Incubator
6 West County Street, Suite 106
Hampton, VA 23663
Contact: Ms. Andrea Thompson
Tel/Fax: (757) 728-9671
Email: profit6@pilot.infi.net

Write Action Plan Notes

Virginia   Group Enterprise Development
                                  (formerly   Ethiopian   Community
                                  Development Council)
                                  1038 S. Highland Street
                                  Arlington, VA 22204
                                  Executive Director: Tschaye Teferra
                                  Microloan Contact: Haddish Welday
                                  E-Mail:
                                  belay.embaye@ECDCinternational.org
                                  Tel: (703) 685-0510
                                  Fax (703) 685-0529
                                  Service Area: Counties of Prince
                                  William, Arlington and Fairfax, and
                                  the Cities of Alexandria and Falls
                                  Church.

Virginia   Lightstone   Community   Development
                                  Corporation
                                  HC 63, Box 73
                                  Moyers, WV 26815
                                  Executive Director: Anthony E. Smith
                                  Microloan Contact: Anthony E. Smith
                                  E-Mail: tony@lightstone.org
                                  Tel: (304) 249-5200
                                  Fax: (304) 249-5310
                                  Service Area: Counties of Bath and
                                  Highland.
                                  Website: http://www.lightstone.org

Virginia   People Incorporated of Southwest
                                  Virginia
                                  1173 West Main Street
                                  Abingdon, VA 24210
                                  Executive   Director: Robert   G.
                                  Goldsmith
                                  Microloan Contact: Phillip Black/Amanda
                                  Fortner Tel: (276-619-2228)
                                  E-Mail: afortner@naxs.com
                                  Tel: (276) 619-2239
                                  Fax: (276) 628-2931

Write Action Plan Notes

Service Area: Counties of Buchanan, Carroll, Dickenson, Grayson, Lee, Russell, Scott, Smythe, Tazewell, Washington, Wise, Wythe, and the Cities of Bristol and Norton.
Website: http://www.peopleincorp.org

Virginia

Richmond Economic Development Corporation
501 E. Franklin Street, Suite 358
Richmond, VA 23219
Program Director: Stephen J. Schley
Microloan Contact: Brenda Lewis
E-mail: sjschley@aol.com
Tel: (804) 780-3013
Fax: (804) 788-4310
Service Area: City of Richmond, Enterprise Zone Areas.

Virginia

Total Action Against Poverty
145 Campbell Avenue, S.W., Suite 303
P.O. Box 2868
Roanoke, VA 24001-2868
Executive Director: Ted Edlich
Microloan Contact: William Skeen
E-Mail: bill.skeen@taproanoke.org
Tel: (540) 345-6781 Ext. 4319
Fax: (540) 343-9892
Service Area: Counties of Alleghany, Bath, Botetourt, Craig, and Roanoke, and the Cities of Clifton Forge, Covington, Roanoke, and Salem.

Virginia

Virginia Community Development Loan Fund
1624 Hull Street
Richmond, VA 23224
Executive Director: Timothy S. Hayes, Sr.

Write Action Plan Notes

Microloan Contact: Janice Fraites
E-Mail: jfraitesvcdlf@earthlink.net
or vcdlf@earthlink.net
Tel: (804) 233-2014
Fax: (804) 233-2158
Service Areas: Counties of Hanover, Henrico, Chesterfield, Goochland, Powatan, and the Cities of Petersburg, and Hopewell.
Website: http://www.vcdlf.org

48 WASHINGTON

MICROLOAN DEMONSTRATION PROGRAM—WASHINGTON

Intermediary Lenders

Washington	Snohomish County Private Industry Council
	728 134th St. SW, Suite A-10, Everett, WA 98204
	Executive Director: Emily Duncan
	Microloan Contact: Roland Chaiton
	E-mail: emily&downhomewa.com
	Tel: (425) 743-9669. Fax: (425) 742-1177
	Service Area: Adams, Chelan, Douglas, Grant, King, Kitsap, Kittitas, Klickitat, Okanogan, Pierce, Skagit, Snohomish, Whatcom, Yakima Counties, and San Juan Island.
Washington	Tri-Cities Enterprise Association
	2000 Logston Boulevard, Richland, WA 99352
	Executive Director: Wilfred Henderson
	Microloan Contact: Katie Fast
	E-mail: dpittock@owt.com/kfast@owt.com

Write Action Plan Notes

Tel: (509) 375-3268. Fax: (509) 375-4838
Service Area: Benton and Franklin counties.

Washington   Washington Association for Minority Entrepreneurs
24 South 3rd Avenue
Yakima, WA 98902
President & CEO: Luz Bazan Gutierrez
Microloan Contact: Luz Bazan Gutierrez
E-mail:
Tel: (509) 453-5133. Fax: (509) 453-5165
Service Area: Mattawa and Othello in Grant County; Moses Lake and Royal City in Adams County; Walla Walla County; and Pasco in Franklin County.

49   WISCONSIN

WISCONSIN SMALL BUSINESS ADMINISTRATION
MICRO LOAN LENDERS AS OF OCTOBER 30, 2003

1   Advocap

Contact: Morton Gazerwitz
19 West First Street, P.O. Box 1108, Fond du Lac, WI 54936
Tel: 920/922-7760. Fax: 920/922-7214
SERVICE AREA : Fond du Lac County.

2   Advocap

Contact: Morton Gazerwitz
2929 Harrison Street, Oshkosh, WI 54901
Tel: 920/426-0150. Fax: 920/426-3071
SERVICE AREA: Winnebago and Green Lake Counties.

Write Action Plan Notes

3   Impact Seven, Inc.

     Contact: William Bay or Mr. Jonathan Anderson
     (MicroLoans)
     147 Lake Almena Drive, Almena, WI 54805
     Tel: 715/357-3334. Fax: 715/357-6233
     SERVICE AREA: Statewide with the exceptions of Fond
     du lac, Green Lake, Kenosha, Milwaukee, Ozaukee,
     Racine, Walworth, Waukesha, Washington and Winnebago
     Counties.

4   Impact Seven, Inc.

     Contact: Paul VanAuken
     140 West Wilson Street, Madison, WI 53703
     Tel: 608/251-8450
     SERVICE AREA: Statewide with the exceptions of Fond
     du lac, Green Lake, Kenosha, Milwaukee, Ozaukee,
     Racine, Walworth, Waukesha, Washington and Winnebago
     Counties.

5   Lincoln Neighborhood Redevelopment

     Contact: Matthew Maigatter, SBA Coordinator
     2266 South 13th Street, Milwaukee, WI 53215
     Tel: 414/671-5619
     E-Mail: LNRC@cbgmail.com
     SERVICE AREA: Milwaukee County.

6   Northeast Entrepreneur Fund

     Contact: Bob Voss
     1225 Tower Avenue, Superior, WI 54880
     Tel: 800/422-0374
     SERVICE AREA: Douglas County in Wisconsin

7   WI Women's Business Initiative Corp.

     Contact: Carol N. Maria

Write Action Plan Notes

2745 N. Dr. Martin Luther King Jr. Dr., Milwaukee, WI
53212
Tel: 414/263-5450. Fax: 414/263-5456
or
Contact: Susan Eick
2300 S. Park St., Suite 4, Villager Mall, Madison, WI
53713
Tel: 608/257-5450. Fax: 608/257-5456
SERVICE AREA: Brown, Dane, Dodge, Jefferson, Kenosha,
Milwaukee, Ozaukee, Racine, Rock, Walworth,
Washington and Waukesha Counties.

50 WEST VIRGINIA

MICROLOAN DEMONSTRATION PROGRAM—WEST VIRGINIA

Intermediary Lenders

W. Virginia

The Washington County Council on
Econ. Dev.
Morgantown Area Economic Partnership
Morgantown Airport
140 Hart Field Road,
PO Box 188 Morgantown WV 26507-0188
Executive Director: Malcolm L.
Morgan
Microloan Contact: Don Reinke
E-mail: info@morgantown.org
Tel: (304) 296-6684. Fax: (304)
296-6689
Service Area: Preston and
Monongalia Counties.

W. Virginia

Mountain CAP of West Virginia, Inc.
105 Jerry Burton Drive, Sutton, WV
26601
Microloan Contact: Tara Rexroad
Tel: (304) 765-7738. Fax (304) 765-
7308
E-mail: tprmtcap@rtol.net

Write Action Plan Notes

Service Area: Barbour, Braxton, Clay, Fayette, Gilmer, Lewis, Nicholas, Randolph, Roane, Upshur And Webster Counties.

W. Virginia

Lightstone Community Development Corporation
HC 63, Box 73, Moyers, WV 26815
Microloan Contact: Michelle Marshall
Email: lfi@lightstone.org
Tel: (304) 249-5200. Fax: (304) 249-5310
Service Area: West Virginia.

Write Action Plan Notes

EXPANDING BUSINESSES

Business Promotion Grants
Equity Capital
Trade Financing

USDA RURAL BUSINESS COOPERATIVE SERVICES

US Department of Agriculture programs to promote business and economic development in rural America.

Types of USDA Loans & Grant Programs:

- **Business and Industry Guaranteed Loans (B&I Guar.):**

The Business and Industry (B&I) Guaranteed Loan Program helps create jobs and stimulates rural economies by providing financial backing for rural businesses. This program provides guarantees up to 80 percent of a loan made by a commercial lender. Loan proceeds may be used for working capital, machinery and equipment, buildings and real estate, and certain types of debt refinancing.

- **Intermediary Relending Program (IRP):**

The purpose of the Intermediary Relending Program (IRP) is to finance business facilities and community development projects in rural areas.

- **Rural Business Enterprise Grants:**

The Rural Business-Cooperative Service (RBS) makes grants under the Rural Business Enterprise Grants (RBEG) Program to public bodies, private nonprofit corporations, and Federally-recognized Indian Tribal groups to finance and facilitate development of small and emerging private business enterprises located in any area other than a city or

Write Action Plan Notes

town that has a population of greater than 50,000 inhabitants and the urbanized area contiguous and adjacent to such a city or town.

- **Rural economic Development/Business Opportunity Grants:**

The purpose is to promote sustainable economic development in rural communities with exceptional needs

Contact the USDA General Service center online to get your servicing center telephone number and address location in your city or State.

The USDA Services center locator is located on the website at http://www.usda.gov. Access to retrieve your servicing center city or state.

Write Action Plan Notes

SMALL BUSINESS INVESTMENT COMPANIES (SBIC) EQUITY FINANCING

Inside the Investment Division of the SBA, the mission is to encourage private risk taking and to expand the reach of venture capital to thousands of small businesses across America.

SBA's Investment Division is responsible for managing both the Small Business Investment Company (SBIC) and New Markets Venture Capital (NMVC) programs. The NMVC program is a pilot program, which supplements the contribution of the much larger SBIC program in bringing investment capital to economically underserved urban and rural areas.

Small business investment companies (SBICs) exist to supply equity capital, long-term loans and management assistance to qualifying small businesses.

The privately owned and operated SBICs use their own capital and funds borrowed from the U.S. Small Business Administration (SBA) to provide financing to small businesses in the form of equity securities and long-term loans.

SBA puts its confidence in premier venture capital funds to evaluate and invest in promising small companies.

Whether your business is in the early stages of development or already thriving and seeking growth capital, the SBIC will help you determine if venture capital financing is right for your company,—remember, the SBIC is the nation's largest fund of funds.

Entrepreneurs have three sources to search for active SBICs. The first is the SBIC directory—a U.S. map on the SBIC homepage at www.sba.gov/inv. Just click on the state or states where your company is located.

Write Action Plan Notes

SBIC Investment Types

1. Seed Financing
This may involve product development and market research as well as building a management team and developing a business plan.

2. Early Stage
This capital is for companies that require funds to initiate full-scale manufacturing and sales.

3. Expansion Financing
This working capital is for companies initiating on expansion in sectors of producing and shipping, its growing accounts receivable and inventories are prime assets as collateral. Although if the company has not shown an aggressive development or showing a profit, this product serves that purpose.

4. Later Stage Financing
This capital is ideally for major expansion of a company whose sales volume is increasing or its 3 quarter projections are profitable. Funds are used for further plant expansion, marketing, working capital or development of an improved product.

5. MBO/LBO/Acquisition
This capital acquisition financing enables companies to fund the finance on acquisition of another company.

Ensuring maximum participation of private financing sources is critically important to the objectives of the SBIC program.

For further information about these programs, please call the SBA Office of Communications and Public Liaison at (202) 205-6444 or send an e-mail to sbic@sba.gov.

Write Action Plan Notes

ACE-Net is another equity finance tool—the SBA's angel capital network, this resource tool electronically matches and brings qualified private investors' vested interest capital to small businesses.

For further information on ACE-Net and Equity financing, we recommend you to visit www.bankrate.com/brm/default.asp.

Write Action Plan Notes

TRADE FINANCING

Making the Government work for you reduces the countless demands and guaranty factor for the loan distribution to emerging companies. Advice and assistance are available to companies at little or no cost.

Assistance is available through federal, state, and local government agencies, as well as the private sector.

Assistance Sources

The Trade Information Center, U.S. Department of Commerce

The Trade Information Center (TIC) is an excellent source for export assistance. The TIC operates the toll free 1-800-USA-TRADE (1-800-872-8723) number for the Department of Commerce and is a comprehensive resource for information on federal export assistance programs.

Export Assistance Centers, U.S. Department of Commerce

The U.S. and Commercial Service (the Commercial Service) of the Department of Commerce has developed and maintains a network of international trade specialists in the United States to help American companies export their products and conduct business abroad.
Please see http://www.doc.gov.

Overseas Posts, U.S. Department of Commerce

Commercial Service officers are working in 67 countries (with 127 offices) and have a personal understanding of local market conditions and business practices.

Trade Development, U.S. Department of Commerce

To assist U.S. businesses in their export efforts, TD's industry and international experts conduct executive

Write Action Plan Notes

trade missions, trade fairs, product literature centers, marketing seminars, and business counseling.

For further information, contact Trade Development, Room 3832, U.S. Department of Commerce, 14th and Constitution Avenue, N.W., Washington, D.C. 20230.

The Advocacy Center, U.S. Department of Commerce

For a U.S. company bidding for a foreign government procurement contract, exporting today can mean more than just selling a good product at a competitive price.

For more information, call 202-482-3896, fax 202-482-3508; Internet home page: http://www.ita.doc.gov/td/advocacy.

Write Action Plan Notes

Organizations offering Trade Finance Programs.

1. **Commerce Department Financing and Grants:** The Department of Commerce helps access project financing and grants for exports companies. Contact the Trade Information center (TIC) 1 800-USA-TRADE for programs guidelines

2. **SBA Export Working Capital Guarantees:** The program encourages lenders to offer export working capital loans by guaranteeing repayment of up to $1 million or 90 percent of a loan amount, whichever is less. For contact information refer to the insert SBA PLP and CLP Lenders by State.

3. **Export Import Bank Financing (Ex-Im):** Export-Import Bank of the United States. 811 Vermont Avenue, N. W. Washington, DC 20571 Tel: 202-565-3946 (EXIM) or 1-800-565-3946 (EXIM). Email: info@exim.gov

4. **Forfaiting:** An alternative potentially to export credit or insurance cover. For further information visit http://www.afia-forfaiting.org.

Write Action Plan Notes

COMMERCIAL BUSINESSES

Surety Bond Guarantees
International Trade Loans
Export Express

SBA's SURETY PROGRAM

Business Contractors engaging in numerous industrial sectors, this is a suitable capital-funding program to fund starting and ongoing contractual projects.

Types of Surety Program

1. **Bid**: Bond which guarantees that the bidder on a contract will enter into the contract and furnish the required payment and performance bonds

2. **Payment**: Bond that guarantees payment from the contractor of money to persons who furnish labor, materials equipment and/or supplies for use in the performance of the contract.

3. **Performance**: Bond which guarantees that the contractor will perform the contract in accordance with its terms.

4. **Ancillary:** Bonds which are incidental and essential to the performance of the contract.

For further information on your local SBA Serving office, contact the Washington, DC District Office. **Address:** 1110 Vermont Avenue, NW.9th Floor. Washington, D.C. 20005. Tel: 202-606-4000.

Write Action Plan Notes

INTERNATIONAL TRADE LOANS

Commercial business preparing to engage in or is already engaged in international trade, the International Trade Loan Program is suitable for your capital needs.

The SBA can guarantee up to $1,250, 000 for a combination of fixed-asset (facilities and equipment) financing and Export Working Capital Program (EWCP) assistance.

The proceeds of a SBA International Trade loan may be used to acquire, construct, renovate, modernize, improve or expand facilities and equipment to be used in the United States to produce goods or services involved in international trade, and to develop and penetrate foreign markets.

Contact the SBA Lenders on the list for a loan application.

EXPORT EXPRESS

For commercial business needing a quick capital source, the SBA Export Express business lending assistance with its technical assistance programs helps commercial businesses that have traditionally had difficulty in obtaining adequate export financing. The pilot program is available nationwide and is expected to run through September 30, 2005.

The SBA Export Express helps commercial businesses that have exporting potential, but need funds to buy or produce goods, and/or to provide services, for export. The funding process is fast and quick.

Contact the SBA Microloan Lender on the list for a quick application.

Write Action Plan Notes

About the Author

Martex E-Technology LLC is a registered Maryland State company, limited by liabilities we operate and engage in transactions on a day-to-day basis. The Department of Assessments and Taxation issued a certificate of Good Standings in coverage of continual business revenue processes and transactions. As an accreditation to us, we made the certificate of good standings a harness to our website at a click of a button, re-instating and reaffirming our mission statements as the network pioneers at the click of a button. We are sub-divisional to handle revenue transactions at www.m-etechllc.com, an e-commerce online store; www.demand-transient.net, the No. 1 Demand-Transient Global Commerce Offline Store in precision to our Customers Storage Solution purchases and BETA Information Technology Value-Added Procurements. CheckTron™ Version 2.06® our B2B payment check processor; a Check 21 Legislation hardware comes with an intuitive out of a box experience OOBE software, it increases better storage utilization. DBA: M-ETECH. business virtues discloses us as the network pioneer limited liability company truncating our transactions with numerous global legacy companies success stories.

Martex E-Technology LLC DBA: M-ETECH. operates in Maryland, Pennsylvania and the United Kingdom. With to our commercial expansion, we will be operating geographically with concise economic markets to the demand-transient of our clients. Visit www.m-etechllc.com, click on e-commerce to view some of the entrepreneurs products available for our partner program. Take your time to register for the ME-TECH Demand-Transient Retailer and E-Tailer Partner Program®.

Hence *Business Financing Commence 1.1*, the business and consumer financial answers solve the entry of capital acquisitions in every state and city in the United States of America. In other words, we rewrote the wheel of business revenue to make you a satisfied corporate and commercial statutory entrepreneur.

Private and Public Enquiries

Head Office.

Martex E-Technology LLC
1735 Market St. Suite A423
Philadelphia, PA 19103-7588
United States of America
Tel: 1 800 959-4806
Fax: 1 814 690-1581
Website: www.m-etechllc.com
Email: author@m-etechllc.com

Administration Centre.

DBA: M-ETECH.
Rosden House
Dept 257
372 Old Street
London
EC1V 9LT
United Kingdom
Tel: ++44 207-060-1889
Fax: ++44 870-135-7637
Website: www.m-etech.com
Email: admin@m-etech.com

ME-TECH.

MARTEX E-TECHNOLOGY LLC. DBA: M-ETECH
D&B D-U-N-S Number: 364801923

978-0-595-38940-7
0-595-38940-6